Performance Management

CRONER © CCH

Croner.CCH Group Limited
145 London Road
Kingston upon Thames
Surrey KT2 6SR
Tel: 020 8547 3333

Published by
Croner.CCH Group Limited
145 London Road
Kingston upon Thames
Surrey KT2 6SR
Tel: 020 8547 3333

First published August 2000

British Library cataloguing in Publication Data. A CIP Catalogue Record for this book is available from the British Library

ISBN 1 85524 583 3

Printed by Creative Print and Design Group Ltd, Wales

CONTRIBUTORS

THE AUTHOR

PETER DOWNES was a comprehensive school headteacher for 21 years, including 14 as Head of Hinchingbrooke School in Huntingdon, Camdridgeshire, a pilot for local funding of schools. He is now an educational consultant. A former President of the Secondary Heads Association, he is now their School Funding Consultant and is working on the reform of the national funding system. He is an accredited external assessor for the Threshold Assessment process and an approved Governor Trainer for Performance Management. He is a regular contributor to Croner's Head's Legal Guide and School Governors' Manual. He is Consultant Editor of the Financial Management for Schools Manual. As part of the Croner Training programme, he leads training days on financial management and on governor training.

THE REVIEWER

Dr CHRIS J NICHOLLS has been Head of Moulsham High School for ten years. He is a member of the executive and council of SHA and is currently pay and conditions officer. He has had published a number of scientific papers, a book on school leadership and articles in education magazines.

He is a consultant for various organisations specialising in improving the performance of boys and performance management.

Contents

INTRODUCTION

As the new century opens, Performance Management (PM) will be a dominant theme of life for teachers, heads and governors in schools all around England and Wales,. This pocket book has been written specifically to guide Governors through PM, to help them to know what they have to do, and, just as importantly, what they do *not* have to do, and to give them an understanding of what is happening in the schools for which they are responsible and in the professional life of the teachers on whom the success of the school depends.

Inevitably, this pocket book will refer to and quote from the many sources of information published by the Department for Education and Employment (DfEE) which is available in schools, but it will go beyond that to interpret and comment so that governors can be aware of the wider implications for them as well as of the specific statutory requirements.

In one sense, PM is extremely simple as a concept. It means giving all members of school staff a clear understanding of what is expected of them, setting monitorable targets, providing the resources and training to enable them to meet those targets, and then holding them to account for their performance. It is not necessarily linked to extra pay although that does form a significant part of the government's plans for the future of the education service.

Although it can be summed up in a simple short paragraph, PM in the context of a school is extremely complex and has profound implications for the way schools are managed. PM enters the educational scene at a moment when public attention is focused more than ever before on educational achievement. The Government sees PM as an essential tool in raising standards and, given that it is a policy which the preceding Government would have liked to introduce but never did, it seems unlikely to be vulnerable to political changes in forthcoming elections. Whether or not the cost implications of the payment element can be sustained in the long term is another matter.

Chapter One looks briefly at how PM fits historically into the development of educational policy. Chapter Two considers how schools might go about putting a PM policy in place, bearing in mind that this is a specific obligation for governors. Chapter Three examines the process of Threshold Assessment in which the governors have no direct role to play, but of which they need to be fully aware. Chapter Four looks at the performance management of the headteacher. Chapter Five examines the training programme for governors which the DfEE will be undertaking during the academic year 2000–2001. The appendices provide supporting material for some of the more technical issues, ie how to measure pupil progress, the new pay structure, the model policy with commentary, the funding of performance management and the threshold assessment criteria.

It is no exaggeration to say that the introduction of PM into schools constitutes a far-reaching change in the terms and conditions of service of teachers and heads. In the opinion of many within the profession, its introduction has been extremely rushed and will suffer from over hasty implementation. The fact remains that the Government intends to proceed with this major reform and it is the responsibility of all concerned to see that it is implemented effectively, drawing from it any merits it may have and seeking to minimise the possible disadvantages.

The other significant factor which needs to be taken into consideration by those who might be tempted to dismiss Performance Management as "just another Government initiative" is the major input of funds to support the whole operation. Not only has there been a promise of £1 billion extra to fund the extra payments for teachers which are at the heart of the programme, but funds have also been made available for training and to provide cover for the time taken to implement the policy. Of the extra funding, £5 million is specifically for the training of governors. This is in marked contrast to many other initiatives in recent years when the teaching profession and governors felt that they were being expected to respond to new requirements but without the time or money to meet the expectations.

It therefore seems sensible for governors to approach this new development in a positive frame of mind, notwithstanding some of the reservations they may have. I hope that the contribution of this particular publication will be supportive to governors by alerting them to possible difficulties but always emphasising the positive outcomes which may emerge over time.

This pocket book has been prepared as training takes place and details of the procedures amended. Please check against official publications in any areas of uncertainty. For the latest information, consult the DfEE website at *www.dfee.gov.uk/teachingreforms*. Two short videos ar available in schools, The *Teaching Reforms* gives an overview and the other one is specifically on the *Threshold Assessment*.

The High Court decision in favour of the NUT's claim that the Secretary of State had acted illegally in imposing threshold Assessment may cause some delay to the time-scales referred to in this pocket-book. It is however extremely unlikely that there will be any major change to the overall policy on Performance Management and the principles on which it is based are likely to remain the same.

CHAPTER 1

RAISING STANDARDS AND REWARDING PERFORMANCE — THE UNFOLDING AGENDA

AS IT WAS IN THE BEGINNING

As we look back to schools in the early 1980s, it is remarkable how relatively unregulated they seem. Apart from the requirement to teach religious education, schools could set up their own curriculum, within the broad but non-statutory expectation that everybody would study English and maths, together with some or all of science, humanities, languages, creative, artistic and practical subjects, and physical education. Within the classroom, teachers were free to do mainly what they wanted and teach in whichever way seemed right to them, based on a largely unwritten consensus about good practice. Inspection of classroom performance was infrequent, carried out mainly by Local Education Authority (LEA) inspectors (most of whom were simultaneously being advisers) and occasionally by Her Majesty's Inspectors (HMI). It was possible for teachers to go for years, even an entire career, without a serious scrutiny of their performance.

Professional consensus guided what happened in schools. There were no conditions of service laying down exactly what teachers should do or how many hours they should spend in school. Even holders of promoted posts had very sketchy job descriptions, if any. Details of a headteacher's post rarely stretched to more than one side of A4. Everybody instinctively knew what was expected of a head, a head of department or a classroom teacher.

INCREASING CENTRAL GOVERNMENT CONTROL

First came the *Terms and Conditions of Service Document* which, for the first time, specified the number of hours each year for which a teacher's activities could be directed. It went on to lay out what teachers are required to do in the 1,265 hours where they are under the direction of the head. The National Curriculum laid down what was to be taught, both in terms of the overall balance of the curriculum and in the detail of each subject. Programmes of study were put in place so that teachers knew explicitly what they were supposed to teach.

Having created a more directed overall structure, it became self-evident that somebody should check up on teachers to see that they were toeing the line. So the inspection regime was strengthened by the creation of the Office for Standards in Education (OFSTED). Teams of inspectors descended upon schools and subjected them to detailed scrutiny, involving not only observation of classroom teaching but consultation with parents and governors by questionnaires and meetings. The publication of the OFSTED report to all parents, raised the stakes for schools. The pronouncements of the Chief Inspector, at times worded in an abrasive style, seemed to symbolise the punitive nature of the inspection regime. More recently, the Framework for Inspection has been lightened, schools which are deemed to be doing well are visited less frequently and the lengthy neurosis-inducing lead-in time has been shortened.

National testing at 7, 11 and 14 years old was added to the pre-existing public examination system for pupils of 16 and over. Schools' results started to be published in the national press. The role of Governors was greatly strengthened by successive pieces of legislation, as was the requirement for them to report to parents through an Annual Report and the Annual Meeting. Standards in schools became a matter of national debate and "raising standards" took on an increasingly political dimension. Education played a prominent role in the 1997 election although it will never be possible to estimate the extent to which the public at large voted for Labour candidates because of the "education, education, education" mantra.

RAISING STANDARDS

The Labour government elected in 1997 intensified the drive for higher standards, accountability and central direction. National strategies for literacy and numeracy, specifying in great detail what should be taught and how, have come to dominate primary schools. As testing has worked its way through the system and the collection of data has become technically easier, the setting of targets at all levels in schools has played a major role. The achievement of higher standards has received the supreme endorsement of Government by the offer (or threat) of the resignation of the Secretary of State for Education and Employment if certain national targets are not met nationally by 2002. The most prominent, that 80% of 11 year olds should be achieving Level 4 in the KS2 English tests (a level achieved by slightly less than half in 1994), has come to dominate the life of primary school classes in Years 5 and 6.

Standards within the teaching profession are no longer left to chance. Those entering teaching have to meet detailed criteria in their training programme. The idea that the PGCE year was a relatively relaxed transition from a degree course to a teaching post has gone forever. Success in numeracy, literacy and ICT tests is a requirement for all teachers. In their first post Newly Qualified Teachers (NQTs) are observed, supported and reported on according to a national framework. Later on in a teaching career, those wishing to proceed to headship now have to follow a tightly prescribed programme and will soon have to achieve the National Professional Qualification for Headship (NPQH). This rapid overview of educational trends of the last decade or so indicates how everything has been moving towards central direction. The Prime Minister acknowledged this as a policy commitment during his Romanes lecture in Oxford in December 1999,

> "For most of the last 150 years, mass education has been of at best fitful concern to England's political leaders, left and right. In consequences, central government has taken scant interest in standards and investment, too often dismissing as a matter of local concern and regulation what was in truth a chronic failure of national leadership and responsibility."

This gives the clearest possible indication that from now on central government is going to take the lead in developing the country's educational system. Exactly how this will work out in terms of the balance of responsibilities between LEAs, governors and heads is still a matter of conjecture. The outcome of a consultation on this balance of responsibilities will be known late in 2000.

TACKLING TEACHER PERFORMANCE

Within this overall trend of centrally imposed and specific requirements, successive governments have found it difficult to get to grips with regulating the quality of the daily performance of teachers on which the success of the whole programme ultimately depends. The marketplace philosophy of the Thatcher era encouraged schools to become better so as to attract more pupils and thereby more money, but this pressure for higher standards was not easily transferable into the classroom.

The 1991 version of appraisal

The classroom teacher, in daily contact with a few or many pupils, is at the heart of the educational process. The government's aspirations for higher standards depend on a consistently better performance by 450,000 individuals in widely differing circumstances. Control at this level has proved elusive. The first attempt was the appraisal regulations for teachers which became law in 1991. This system of appraisal was the subject of prolonged negotiation with the teacher unions and associations who vigorously protected their members from any hint of a judgemental appraisal. The whole process was built on the concept of developmental appraisal, usually by a peer, rather than an assessment of performance carried out by a line manager.

In the early days, INSET days were set aside for the implementation of this procedure and money was made available to release teachers to take part. Gradually that funding disappeared and appraisal fell into limbo, not least because there were inadequate training funds to meet the developmental needs which had been identified. In recent years most schools had abandoned the former appraisal system even though the regulations were technically in force until September 2000.

The Green Paper 1999

The 1999 Green Paper, *Teachers — Meeting the Challenge of Change*, marked a significant change of direction. Emboldened by a buoyant economy that enabled the Government to back some of its proposals with the prospect of extra money, the DfEE announced its intention of modernising the profession by introducing Performance Management as a permanent dimension of school life. There was a massive consultation exercise across the country and over 40,000 written responses were received, said to be the highest response ever received to a Green Paper. There was considerable hostility to the proposals: some objected to the link between pay and judgment in relation to the crossing of a threshold to an upper pay range; others were concerned about the potentially divisive effect of what might be perceived as first and second class teachers; some were concerned about the funding of the proposals and particularly about what may happen after the first two years have passed; even those who were broadly sympathetic to the concepts felt that it was being introduced on too short a time-scale.

Having taken note of the comments made and being particularly aware of the need to avoid unnecessary bureaucracy, the government pressed ahead. A whole army had to be recruited to implement the programme — lead trainers, trainers, external assessors, external advisers, performance management consultants, writers and all the administrative back-up. All 24,500 headteachers received a day's training in late March and early April, facilitated by accredited assessors who had themselves been trained only days before. A further half day of training was made available in late June and early July.

The logistics of this entire exercise and the financial investment required to make them happen for example, cover for time off school, accommodation expenses, remuneration for trainers, materials (including videos for every headteacher), give a clear indication of the seriousness of the government's intentions and the urgency they attached to the enterprise.

PERFORMANCE RELATED PAY (PRP) IN SCHOOLS

In one sense, the performance of teachers has always been a significant factor in salary increases. Teachers have achieved higher salaries by taking responsibility points (now renamed management allowances) for specific extra responsibilities — a curriculum or Key Stage co-ordinator in a primary school, a head of department or faculty or a Year Head in a secondary school. One of the factors that appointing bodies would take into consideration when allocating these supplementary cash payments would have been the classroom performance of the applicants, but it would not have been tightly measured, largely because the data tools have only recently become available. Receiving extra pay for taking on extra responsibilities was not perceived by the teaching profession to be PRP as such although, in practice, it had a large PRP element.

Those wishing to achieve even higher salaries within a school setting have been required to go through the route of promotion to deputy head and to headteacher. The differential in remuneration between heads, deputies and classroom teachers is substantial and more than in other countries. In France, for example, where pay is related to the quality of the original teaching qualification, to seniority and to inspection, it is not infrequent for a classroom teacher to be receiving a higher salary than a headteacher.

The present structure in English schools, the Government has said, is flawed because it takes the best teachers out of the classroom and rewards management skills above teaching skills. In practice, most teachers receiving extra points for responsibilities still have a very full teaching timetable. In most primary schools deputy heads have a full class responsibility. In secondary schools, heads of department might typically have a period or two for departmental administration but could hardly be said to have abandoned the classroom. Even in some of the largest secondary schools, many heads and deputies continue to teach, usually from choice but also, in some areas of the country, because of financial pressures. The head who is purely an administrator remote from the day-to-day cut and thrust of school life is the exception rather than the rule. Although the Government's basic contention, ie that higher salaries means the abandonment of teaching, is untrue, they have insisted on proceeding with a new structure which relates pay more directly to classroom performance.

WHAT HAPPENS IN OTHER COUNTRIES?

Comparisons with other countries are difficult to make because the status and conditions of teachers are very different. In many European countries, for example, teachers have the status of civil servants which gives them a measure of protection but also puts them in the position of having to go where the state directs them. In her chapter in *Performance-Related Pay in Education,* Joanna Le Métais, a specialist in European education systems concludes:

> "Although the trend towards accountability in education is growing throughout Europe, there is little evidence of performance-related pay other than that resulting from promotion to a more senior post or scale."

It is to the USA that we might look for greater experimentation in pay structures. There, the lack of a national system, the multiplicity of school districts, the greater freedom for administrators to create their own systems in response to local needs have enabled PRP schemes to be tried out. Writing in *Performance-Related Pay in Education,* Dr. Stephen Jacobson, whose doctoral thesis was on "Alternative practices of internal salary distribution and their effects on teacher recruitment and retention", reports that in the 1920s, 40% of American school districts had "merit plans" in effect. Through the century these schemes declined in number because they were found to be unworkable, or there was insufficient money, or union opposition killed them. By the end of the century, the number of teachers receiving some form of performance pay had fallen to about 2%. The criteria used were varied:

- a bonus for all teachers in a school where the academic outcomes in standardised achievement tests were above expectation
- Extra pay for teaching educationally disadvantaged students
- extra pay for teaching shortage subject
- a bonus for undertaking in-service training
- a reward for not being absent.

Jacobson concludes that,

> "although there is little to encourage the belief that performance-related pay plans can effectively improve teacher performance, advocates of merit pay in the USA are probably correct when they argue that the US public would be more willing to support higher teacher salaries if salary increases were somehow pegged to improved student performance."

Performance-Related Pay in Education was published in 1992 in the aftermath of the 1991 appraisal negotiations. The arguments it contains have new relevance today and the book offers valuable insights into the basic issues underlying the measurement of teacher performance. The book's editor, Harry Tomlinson, now Professor of Educational Management at Leeds Metropolitan University, concluded the final chapter with words which now appear to have been prophetic:

> "Without paying for high-quality performance, there will not be the significant further improvement in standards which is absolutely essential. What is needed is the determination by governors and

> headteachers to use the pay policy to improve performance. If this is not achieved, pay will continue to decline relative to national averages. The present system of paying teachers for having a responsibility regardless of how successfully they carry it out, for qualifications often achieved many years previously regardless of whether they have been updated, for having experience without evaluating whether it is leading to improved quality, and without any judgment as to the quality of performance , [all this] is distinctly unprofessional, indeed arguably pretty amateurish."

PRP IN CONTEXT

Teachers who have complained about the prospect of performance management in schools are frequently met with scorn by people working in other professional and commercial worlds where PRP is commonplace. Leaving aside the exceptional cases where top people's earnings are directly related to company profitability or share-holdings, in many enterprises there is a line-managed assessment of performance at all levels. This usually results in a five point scale of judgment, on which a salary increase depends.

Appraisal linked to PRP is accepted as a normal part of everyday business and professional life. In some cases, there is no money to fund any increase arising from the appraisal and then the scheme falls into disrepute and is abandoned. Some argue that it makes no difference because the bonus or pay increase is too small to act as an incentive. Others believe it to be demeaning to a professional person to be judged in this way. Yet others see it as a necessary component of quality. In some companies it has been abandoned because it worked against team spirit and led to disharmony. One of the more telling stories on the management conference circuit is of a company whose first PRP scheme gave bonuses to those staff with the biggest sales figures. Because there were so few winners, the scheme failed to motivate. Then they had the idea of calling all the sales reps together to share their tips for increasing sales. At the end of the day, all the reps voted for the best idea they had picked up during the day and this attracted the prize. In this way all the company reps shared good ideas, the turnover of the firm improved, all the reps got enhanced profit-related bonuses and the shareholders were pleased too.

"SCHOOLS ARE NOT BUSINESSES"

The similarities and differences between schools and the world of business have been frequently aired. In the school context, the "product" is largely intangible (ie rounded, well-educated, socially conscious and hard-working individuals) and there is no direct profit motive. Advocates of PRP allege that this argument has been too long used to protect teachers from a thorough scrutiny of their individual effectiveness. Not having some form of PRP discourages the conscientious, it is said, because they see the idlers in the staff room getting the same pay as the really hard workers. Some late entrants to teaching come into the profession from a business background precisely because they wish to escape the hard-nosed and competitive element inherent in pursuing profit.

The contrary view is that, while schools do not have the commercial incentive of a typical business, they would benefit from a more business-like approach. This is where governors with a wider experience of the business world will be able to make a useful contribution to the discussion.

THE INCREASED AVAILABILITY OF PERFORMANCE DATA

The significant change in recent years has been the explosion of data which enables the academic performance of individual pupils to be tracked in much more detail than ever before. This will be discussed further in Chapter 3 and in Appendix 1. It is a matter of some debate as to whether the extent of the data and its mastery across the teaching profession is such in 2000 as to make the performance management process statistically robust.

Some critics of the Government's proposals argue that it will be another two years before the data collection is sufficiently established to allow judgements at individual teacher level to be made. In other words, whatever the rights and wrongs of appraisal and PRP in principle, the Government is simply moving too fast.

This Government, like any other, has its political imperatives, its electoral time-scale and the potential of its cash-flow. These considerations no doubt contribute to the breathtaking pace at which this fundamental change is being introduced.

BETTER REWARDS AND THE RECRUITMENT OF TEACHERS

The Government has also had to face up to the very serious problem of the shortfall in teacher recruitment. This has been particularly serious in certain subject areas in the secondary sector (modern languages, sciences, technology) and in the recruitment of men in both secondary and primary sectors. An indication of the seriousness of the situation has been the government's decision, from September 2000, to make a payment of £6000 to PGCE students, enhanced by a further £4,000 to those teachers in shortage subjects who are still in post at the beginning of their second year of teaching. The PM proposals are an attempt to make the teaching profession not only more financially attractive, but also to increase its status. Added to this is the creation from September 2000 of the General Teaching Council. All these measures, together with advertising campaigns, are aimed at boosting the self-esteem of teachers and the attractiveness of teaching as a profession. Whether this can compete with the even greater financial attractions of the world of commerce and industry remains to be seen.

RECOMMENDED READING

- *Performance-Related Pay in Education*, Harry Tomlinson, published by Routledge, (1992)

CHAPTER 2

PERFORMANCE MANAGEMENT: THE GOVERNMENT'S PROGRAMME

The DfEE publication *Performance Management Framework* (DfEE ref: 0051/2000) (the *Framework*) has been in all schools since April 2000 and lays out very clearly the Government's belief that Performance Management will help "schools improve by supporting and improving teachers' work, both as individuals and in teams".

The wording is significant because it seeks to emphasise the positive and minimise the negative. The instinctive reaction of many teachers has been a fear that they are being judged because the profession is seen to be failing. The Chief Inspector's remarks that there are 15,000 failing teachers in the country had a devastating effect on morale. By not saying that there are 435,000 teachers who are at least satisfactory and probably good or very good, the Chief Inspector created a climate of demoralisation which has had knock-on effects on retention and recruitment in the teaching profession.

The reference to "in teams" also helps to dispel the myth that PM is divisive and will set teacher against teacher. The PM process is not intended to produce a pecking-order of good and less good teachers within a school; it is intended to raise the standards of all teachers for even those who are doing well can always find ways of doing even better.

The *Framework* goes on to highlight two major benefits:

1. Pupils will benefit because their teachers will have a more sharply focused picture of what, with encouragement, support and high expectations, their pupils can achieve.
2. Teachers will benefit. Teachers have the right to expect that their performance will be regularly assessed and that they will have a proper opportunity for professional discussion with their team leader about their work and professional development.

The reaction of many teachers and governors will be "we are doing that already". No teacher sets out on his day's work with the conscious intention of discouraging pupils or of depressing standards. Many schools already have systems in place by which teachers can reflect on their work with senior colleagues and can have a productive discussion of their professional development needs.

The *Framework* wisely recognises that there is already much good practice in schools. What this initiative is basically doing is trying to enshrine existing best practice in law so that it is obligatory in all schools. By writing down objectives and formalising the procedures, teachers and schools become more self-consciously explicit about what they are doing.

Explicit and formal procedures do also have the potential downside of becoming a mere formality, just another administrative hoop to jump through. Setting objectives in writing can also be limiting because it forces people to concentrate on specific areas and possibly neglect others which are equally valid. The most obvious example is that a heavy over-emphasis on narrow academic results could lead a school to neglect extra-curricular activities or the wider personal and social development of pupils.

This is where governors have a role to play in monitoring the effect of the PM policy on the school over time. They will have the strategic oversight and will be able to pick up from their informal contacts with teachers and parents just how much the school is being affected by the policy, for good or for evil.

The DfEE framework emphasises five key features of a good PM policy. The first three are self-evidently good and uncontentious:

- Raising standards for all pupils.
- Stimulating continuous professional development.
- Involving teachers in school planning and in mutual help and support.

The next two key works highlight areas where the overview of governors may prove to be helpful:

- Manageability — so that performance management is regarded as an integral and essential part of how the school operates.
- Equity — to ensure policies and processes are open and fair, while respecting confidentiality to individuals.

The Governors will clearly have a role in seeing that the whole process is manageable. As with all innovations, performance management is likely to be uppermost in people's minds in 2000–2001. Innovations, especially those which are legally binding and demanding, can easily "take over" school life. Some years ago the introduction of Local Management of Schools and School Development Planning had such an effect. The wise governing body will try to see that the policy is implemented in a balanced and reasonable way. For example, an over-burdensome classroom observation mechanism should be avoided.

Equity is an intangible quality but an important one if relations within a staff room are not to be soured. The reality of life is that not everyone gets on equally well with all colleagues and there is the danger that a performance management policy could be misused for the settling of old scores, for harassment of less popular teachers or the favouring of the popular. This is a sensitive area where the governors will need to "pick up the vibes" so that misuse of the process can be avoided.

THE TIMESCALE FOR IMPLEMENTATION

It is the Government's intention that Performance Management policies should be established in all schools during the Autumn term 2000, that head teachers should have had objectives set by 31 December 2000 and that all teachers should have been set objectives by 28 February 2001. This is a tight timescale but strenuous efforts are being made in terms of investment of time and money to see that it happens. For the first year the cycle can be set at any period between 9 months and 18 months for teachers. Thereafter, the cycle is an annual one.

The DfEE expects that the policy will be implemented in schools by a number of people, depending on the size of the school. The framework coins the term *team leader* to designate a person who will be responsible for reviewing the work of up to four or five others, who are called *job holders*. The team leader will probably be the person most closely connected with the job holder on a day-to-day basis, but a school may decide that a person more detached from daily contact may be more objective. In primary schools, a Key Stage co-ordinator or curriculum leader may be well placed to be a team leader. In a secondary school, a head of department or faculty, a member of the leadership group or a head of a pastoral team would seem to be the most appropriate. As it is the head teachers who will be responsible for recommending the pattern of appraisal to the governing body, this is an area where the governors could reasonably ask for an explanation of the basis on which the structure has been created. Those who are team leaders will themselves be appraised as job holders by somebody else. The head teacher will clearly appraise senior colleagues but must be dissuaded from taking on too many appraisals. Where the Guidelines stipulate four or five appraisals per team leader, this should apply to the headteacher as it does to anybody else.

The training and co-ordination of the team leaders will be an essential task of the headteacher as the process unfolds during the autumn term 2000.

THE NATURE AND TIMING OF THE PERFORMANCE MANAGEMENT CYCLE

It is envisaged that the cycle has three stages:

- Planning — at this stage, the team leader discusses with the job holder their priorities and objectives for the coming year. These objectives are written down and there is to be a discussion of how progress will be monitored
- Monitoring — the teacher and team leader keep progress under review throughout the cycle, taking any supportive action needed.
- Review — the team leader and the teacher formally review achievements over the year and evaluate progress against the objectives set.

The exact timing of this cycle, after the implementation phase, is an area of debate to which the governors could contribute. There is no single answer for all schools. Much depends on the pattern of workload within the school and the availability of data which may be part of the review.

For example, in a secondary school, it might seem sensible to hold the reviews in late June and July when the public examinations have been completed and some of the pressure is removed. However, the data from the public exams will not be available until after the holidays. In the secondary school, another possible time for review would be late November/early December. By this time, the public examination data and the Autumn package would be available (see Appendix 1 for a fuller explanation). Any recommendations referring to salary levels should be known to the Personnel and/or Finance Committee before the detailed budget planning takes place in February. On the other hand, a particular school might have a pattern of work which sees December as one of its busiest months with, say, mock examinations and school drama and music productions.

The end of the Autumn term might be an inappropriate one for a primary school which gives high priority to its Christmas programme. In a primary school, and end-of-summer term review, as soon as SAT results are known, might be more sensible, but that can be a time when some primary schools organise school visits and camps so that staff are away for days at a time.

There is no easy answer to the question of the timing of the cycle. It does not have to be identical for every team leader and teacher. Indeed, if a team leader has four colleagues to review, it would seem advisable to space these over a period of time rather than try to do them all in one rush. However, co-ordingating development needs wil always be difficult in such a scheme.

These are matters on which the head teacher will consult staff and governors and arrive at the best solution for the particular school. The strategic overview role of the governors is to help the head keep the whole life of the school in perspective.

Annex B of the Performance Management Framework document gives further examples of the issues to be considered in various schools in planning the review cycle.

THE STATUTORY ROLE OF THE GOVERNING BODY

The establishment of a performance management policy

The Governors' role in Performance Management is a statutory one. The **Education (School Teacher Appraisal) (England) Regulations 2000** (SI No. 1620), coming into force on 1 September 2000, gives the duty to appraise to a governing body in the following terms,

> "It shall be the duty of the governing body of a school to secure that the performance in discharging their duties of school teachers at the school is regularly appraised in accordance with these regulations" [para. 4].

This means that the governing body has to see that the school has a performance management policy in place as early as possible in the Autumn term, 2000. Fortunately it will not have to start from a blank piece of paper. The government has published a model policy (see Appendix 3) which will provide a useful starting point.

In subsequent years, the governing body will receive from the head teacher, at least once each year, a written report about:

- the operation of school teachers' appraisal at the school
- the effectiveness of the appraisal procedures
- the training and developmental needs of the school teachers [para. 16].

The governors are not themselves directly involved in the appraisal of the teachers. Fears among some teachers that appraisal would see governors snooping around classrooms with clipboards can be put firmly to rest.

The appraisal of the head teacher

The governors have a more direct role in the appraisal of the head teacher but not all the governors will be involved:

> "The governing body of a school shall appoint one or more governors to be appraiser or appraisers for the head teacher, and may appoint a new appraiser in place of an existing appraiser at any time." [para. 5 (1)]

The advice emerging from the DfEE is that two or three would normally be an appropriate number for the head teacher appraisal panel. However, there are restrictions on who may be appointed:

> "No governor who is a teacher or other member of staff at the school shall be appointed as appraiser of the head teacher" [para. 5 (2)]

This requirement should not present major difficulties other than in schools with small governing bodies which have a high proportion of staff on the governing body.

A further complication is that as the head teacher has the right of review of his or her appraisal, care must be taken to ensure that an appropriate "review officer" is available:

> "The review officer in relation to a complaint by a head teacher shall be the chairman of the governing body, but where the chairman of the governing body has participated in the appraisal complained of, the governing body shall appoint one or more governors who have not participated in the appraisal complained of as review officer(s) in relation to such complaint" [para. 17 (2)]

This paragraph may be a topic for some debate among the governors because in many schools it will be the chairman who has the most detailed knowledge of the work of the head teacher. This will also guide the governors in the question of training. As we shall see in Chapter Five, it is anticipated that each governing body will send three people to receive the accredited training. Para. 17 (2) suggests that a fourth person would need to attend or at the very least receive some cascaded training in order to be able to carry out the review procedure effectively.

Governors will probably be relieved to know that they can and indeed must call on support in their appraisal of the head teacher,

> "The governing body of a school shall appoint an external adviser in relation to the appraisal of the head teacher, and may appoint a new external adviser in place of an existing external adviser at any time." [para. 6]

The *external adviser* will be chosen by the governors from a list supplied by the contractors who are administering this whole process — Cambridge Education Associates. The advisers on this list will have received training and will have had to be approved before they are put on the list. There will be a pen portrait of each adviser so that the governors can choose somebody who, in their opinion, has relevant experience, both of the phase of school, its socio-economic circumstances and its size. The former head of a large secondary school from the leafy shires would be an unlikely choice to assist with the appraisal of the head of a small primary school in an inner city.

The external adviser must not be anybody who has had a recent connection with the school or the head teacher.

Governors will certainly find the input of the external adviser helpful and we shall consider later what he/she might do in practice but it needs to be remembered that it is the governors' panel which carries out the appraisal and not the external adviser.

A MORE DETAILED LOOK AT THE REVIEW CYCLE

Stage 1: Planning and setting objectives

The cycle begins with a meeting between the teacher (job holder) and the designated team leader. The aim of this meeting is to provide a focus for the teacher's activity in the coming year and to set specific objectives.

The number of objectives, it is suggested, should be not fewer than three and not more than five or six. They should cover the range of the teacher's activities i.e. a teacher who has a curricular or pastoral responsibility should expect to have an objective related to that part of their work. The objectives should also relate to the School Development

Plan or the teacher's individual needs. (This is in contrast to the criteria for the Threshold Assessment, where the emphasis is on classroom performance and not on wider responsibilities see Chapter 3.)

At least one of the objectives should relate to pupil progress. The objectives should relate to a specific group of pupils or, possibly in the case of special needs teachers, to a few named individuals with whom the teacher is working closely. The prior knowledge and performance of the pupils will be taken into account and both the team leader and the teacher will need to be comfortable with the handling of the available data. These might include standardised test scores, previous public examinations results, benchmarking figures from the LEA and OFSTED information. The main point is that the targets should be relevant to the ability of the pupils in the class. Simplistic and crude results say very little about the performance of the teacher. For example, in a secondary school where setting for maths takes place, it is possible for a teacher taking set 3 to achieve better value-added results than the teacher taking set 1 although the raw scores for set 1 may look better. The assessment of pupil progress is looked at in more technical detail in Appendix 1.

Another objective might be related to professional development. This might include the observation of other teachers, being a mentor to a Newly Qualified Teacher (NQT) or to an Initial Teacher Training (ITT) student if the school is linked with a training establishment. It could include studying for a further qualification (M.A, M.Ed or MBA) or, in the case of more senior staff, the training for the National Professional Qualification for Headship (NPQH) might be appropriate. Subject specialists in the secondary sector might be encouraged to become members of their specialist association, to read its publications and to attend meetings and conferences. A good objective might be for the teacher not only to attend such events but to prepare a short report on them for circulation to the other members of the department.

For a teacher with a management allowance, a third objective might relate to the way that responsibility is carried out. A teacher in charge of Information and Communication Technology (ICT) in a primary school might have as a target the extension of the use of ICT by all the teachers in the school. A pastoral leader with a team of tutors in a secondary school might have targets relating to the attendance and behaviour of all the pupils in the year group. A deputy head who does the timetable might have more sophisticated objectives such as achieving no "teacher wastage" (teachers with more free periods than the agreed entitlement because of poor timetabling) or allowing more flexible setting.

The *Framework* stresses that the objectives should be clear and precise, neither too ambitious nor too easy. The adjective "challenging" is suggested for guidance. Teachers who set challenging targets which they narrowly fail to meet should be encouraged in their efforts rather than being allowed to slip into setting easily achievable targets.

The DfEE *Performance Management Framework* document gives in its Annex C a range of examples which governors will be interested to look at. As might be expected from a government publication, they all make it look quite easy and straightforward. In reality, a great deal will depend on the extent to which any given school has collected data in the past and how well the staff have been trained to use it. In 1999, the picture across the country was extremely varied. At one extreme, there are schools which have been doing detailed analysis of pupil input measures and outcomes over several years while others still do not reliable baseline data. LEAs are now able to provide better benchmarking data showing how well a school is doing relative to others in the same authority and in the rest of the country but not all are yet able to do that against a solid shared statistical database.

The teacher's objectives are written up in the *Individual Plan* and a suggested form is provided in the DfEE model policy.

Stage 2: Monitoring progress

It is the Government's intention that the team leader should keep in touch with the teacher's progress during the year and not simply leave it all until the review meeting twelve months later. The form of the monitoring will vary according to circumstances but it is suggested that classroom observation should be part of. Given the well-known phenomenon of a teacher putting on a special lesson for a visit by an inspector, a school's policy might include a reference to the number of lessons to be observed and the prior notice teachers will receive (if any). Classroom observation must have a focus, be carefully recorded (a suggested pro forma is included in the model policy) and there should be constructive feedback within a specified time.

There will be a temptation in the first phase of the implementation of PM to focus on the beginning and the end, ie the objective — setting meeting and the review meeting. If standards are to rise, much will depend on the quality of the in-year monitoring. If, for example, it is realised that the original objectives are hopelessly unrealistic, these can be changed by agreement during the year. If the team leader considers that there are weaknesses to be addressed, this can be done if the monitoring is consistent and supportive.

Stage 3: Reviewing performance

The review at the end of the cycle is an opportunity for a more extended and detailed reflection on the teacher's performance. As with all review procedures, the interview must be carefully prepared by both parties. The team leader will be expected to:

- confirm the essential tasks, objectives and standards of the teacher
- recognise the strengths and achievements of the year
- confirm action agreed during the in-year monitoring
- identify areas for development and how these will be met
- recognise the teacher's personal development needs.

The team leader has to produce a concise statement summarising the review and making a professional judgement about the overall effectiveness of the teacher having taken all aspects of that teacher's work into account. The statement should be written as soon as possible after the review.

This agenda for the review meeting is easy to write in the abstract, but will clearly be difficult to carry out smoothly in all cases. There are going to be differences of opinion between teacher and team leader; where colleagues have been working together in a department for many years, putting one in judgement over another could cause friction. There may be cases where a teacher being appraised by the team leader who is their head of department may feel that their lack of progress is partially caused by the incompetence of the person who is appraising them. That is why the head should think twice before automatically distributing the roles in the most obvious way.

The teacher retains a copy of his or her individual plan and review and a copy goes to the headteacher. If there are implications for professional development, the person responsible for staff training and development should be informed. There is as yet no clear picture as to how much money will be available for the identified development needs. Although the government has set aside funds through the Standards Fund in 2000–2001 for the performance management process, it is not yet clear how the expected demand for further training will be handled. This was one of the weaknesses of the previous appraisal system and it remains to be seen whether this will become the Achilles heel of this current initiative.

HANDLING COMPLAINTS

It is hoped and expected that in the majority of cases the process will go smoothly and with a high degree of professionalism. Where a teacher is dissatisfied with his or her review, the issue can be raised with the head or, when the head is the team leader, with the chair of governors. As we will see in Chapter Four, when the head is dissatisfied and the chair of governors has already been involved in the process, new governors have to be appointed.

A review of the process takes place and a decision made by the "review officer" to retain the existing statement, amend it or scrap it. The headteacher appoints a new team leader but clearly this person is going to be in a difficult position having not been able to monitor the teacher throughout the year.

PERFORMANCE MANAGEMENT AND PAY

The Government has been at pains to point out that there is no direct annual link between the appraisal process and pay. This is why this whole initiative cannot properly be described as the introduction of Performance Related Pay (PRP). Achieving or failing to achieve objectives will not have an immediate link to remuneration.

However, in some circumstances there may be a link and so the Personnel, Finance or Remuneration Committee may need to be informed of a recommendation. With effect from September 2000, teachers below point 9 on the main scale can be awarded a double increment for outstanding performance *(see Appendix 2 for more details)*. Teachers on the Advanced Skills Teacher scale and teachers on the Leadership spine might also be eligible for financial enhancement. Teachers approaching the Threshold Assessment stage in their career *(see Chapter Three)* may well draw on information from performance reviews in submitting their application.

This statement leaves unanswered the key question of affordability. Whereas the Threshold payments are to be specifically funded for two years and the leadership spine enhancements for one *(see Appendix 4)*, there is no suggestion that extra money will be included for double-jumps. The governors may well find themselves in the invidious position of having to weigh the merits of a strong performance review against other school budget pressures. This is where the much-publicised disparity in funding across the country will have a significant part to play. Outstandingly good young teachers in under-funded parts of the country may well not get their due reward.

PERFORMANCE REVIEW AND CAPABILITY PROCEDURES

The Framework stresses that performance review does not form part of disciplinary or dismissal procedures. There is already a national agreement on capability procedures which specify the need for formal oral and written warnings. In fact, very few teachers are subject to capability procedures. In 1999 just over 3000 teachers out of 450,000 faced some form of capability procedure and of those 604 were sacked, retired or resigned.

However, it is self-evident that if the review process, together with other information or, say, parental complaints, gives rise to concern about the capability of the teacher, it may lead to a decision to investigate and record performance more intensively. Where a decision is taken to enter into a formal capability procedure, that supersedes performance management arrangements.

RESTARTING THE CYCLE

The *Framework* suggests that the circle starts again at the review meeting which becomes the planning meeting for the next cycle. It remains to be seen in practice whether that will work satisfactorily. Particularly in the early years of implementation, it is likely that the anxiety surrounding the review meeting may not be conducive to a rational forward planning session and it may be better to leave a few weeks for recovery and perspective.

CONCLUSION

In this chapter we have looked at the performance management process as the government intends it to happen, following closely their published recommendations and adding comments, examples and a few warnings. We all need to recognise that it will not go smoothly all the time — teachers will be absent on key dates, team leaders will fall ill and have long-term absence and some teachers may change post during the year. Governors will need to be fully informed as to how the process is going, but to be realistic in what can be achieved.

The government has set the stakes high and rightly so. To come out with a low expectation model for raising standards would have been derisory. Given the fundamental commitment of people at all levels of the education service to make things work better for the pupils, it is probable that the whole process will eventually have a positive effect but we must not expect perfection overnight.

RECOMMENDED READING

- *Performance Management in Schools, Performance Management Framework,* DfEE April 2000.
- *Performance Management in Schools, Guidance Note,* DfEE April 2000.

Copies of these documents can be obtained by ringing DfEE Publications on 0845 6022260 or e-mail: dfee@prologistics.co.uk. Alternatively, the documents and additional information can be found on the website: *www.dfee.gov.uk/teachingreforms*.

CHAPTER 3

THRESHOLD ASSESSMENT

The implementation of Performance Management has started with "Threshold Assessment". This is a process which enables a classroom teacher to pass from the main pay range on to the upper pay spine *(see Appendix 2)*. The governors are not involved in this process in any way other than that the chair of governors receives a copy of the final report made to the headteacher by the external assessor. Although the governors have no direct part to play, it is important that they know what is happening because of the implications for relationships and practices within the school. Threshold Assessment will also be part of the school's performance management policy for which the governors are ultimately responsible.

ELIGIBILITY, APPLICATION, ASSESSMENT AND FEEDBACK

All teachers who have reached point 9 on the main pay scale, because of their years of experience and qualification, are eligible to apply, including part-time staff and qualified teachers employed not in schools but by LEAs. Teachers in further education (FE) and Sixth Form colleges are not employed under the same terms and conditions and are not eligible.

Teachers apply using a form that is available in the school. When the form is completed, it is handed to the headteacher who has to make a judgment and state that the specified standards have or have not been met. After that, the application forms are forwarded to an external assessor whose task is to verify the judgments made by the headteacher. The external assessor is appointed by the company which is managing the process, (Cambridge Education Associates). This verification is done by reading through all of the applications and making a sample selection for closer scrutiny. The assessor visits the school and checks whether the evidence which supports the details of each application has been examined.

The role of the assessor is to ensure that there is a national adherence to the specified standards. The assessor will corroborate the headteacher's judgment, or challenge some of them and reach a resolution after discussion with the headteacher, or, in extreme circumstances, abort the assessment because he or she is dissatisfied with the evidence provided. The assessor will also discuss with the headteacher the progress the school is making towards the implementation of its performance management policy and will comment on this in the report, of which the chair of governors will receive a copy.

The assessors decision is final and there is no appeal procedure. Teachers who are unsuccessful at their first attempt, or who decide not to apply, can do so in subsequent years. After the verification has been completed, the headteacher holds a debriefing with each applicant, successful and unsuccessful. The purpose of this is to indicate, even with those whose application has been approved, ways in which they could develop in the future.

It is the headteacher who is personally responsible for making the assessment and this cannot be delegated to others. In large schools, it is probable that the headteacher will call on help and information from team leaders, heads of department and senior staff but it is the head who has to make the judgements and manage the process.

THE AIMS OF THRESHOLD ASSESSMENT

The assessment is made against eight criteria grouped in five areas (*see Appendix* 5). The emphasis throughout is on classroom performance rather than on the satisfactory fulfilment of management responsibilities. The government's aims are to:

- reward good classroom teachers
- encourage good classroom teachers to stay in the classroom rather than seek to earn more money by being promoted out of the classroom
- improve recruitment to the profession by showing the government's commitment to high professional standards and to better remuneration for successful practitioners

- raise standards in all schools by making explicit the qualities expected of teachers
- put pressure on schools to implement a performance management policy as rapidly as possible.

IMPLEMENTATION

The implementation of the Threshold Assessment was rushed through. Within weeks of the publication of the School Teachers' Review Body Report, which supported the government's intentions as previously laid out in the Green Paper, hundreds of external assessors had been recruited, trained and accredited. All headteachers were summoned to headteacher training days which were held across the country in a three-week period. This was completed by the end of the Easter term. By 5 June, all teachers wishing to apply for the Threshold Assessment had completed their application. Headteachers had to make their judgments by 31 July. This deadline was extended to 30 October for schools with more than 40 applicants.

The external verification of the process started in the Autumn term 2000 and will be completed by Christmas or shortly afterwards. Teachers who are successful have a pay rise of £2001 backdated to 1 September 2000.

THE FUNDING ARRANGEMENTS

Governors on finance committees may well be worried about the costs to the school budget of the performance management process. They can be reassured that there will be no negative impact in the short term since the government has set aside relatively generous funding to kick-start this policy *(see Appendix 4)*.

In the longer term, it is not yet known how the extra costs will be incorporated into school budgets. The normal mechanism, (through the nationally determined Standard Spending Assessment down to LEAs who then delegate to schools), will need significant amendment if it is not to further disadvantage those schools which are already underfunded.

Simultaneous with the implementation of performance management, the government has launched a wide-ranging consultation on the funding of local government. A Green Paper published in the summer of 2000 offers a number of different ways forward.

LONG-TERM IMPLICATIONS

Although governors have no direct role in the Threshold Assessment process, some of the outcomes will affect their work. For example, they may find themselves on the receiving end of criticism from teachers in their school who have failed to pass through the threshold. The advice would be for individual governors not to get involved in any way with recriminations or post-mortems.

Governors on future appointing panels may well find themselves having to make a choice between sub- and post-threshold teachers. Normally, they would make their judgements in the light of the criteria for the post and the suitability of the candidates but, depending on the long-term financial arrangements, they may also need to take salary into consideration (as they have already had to do in some cases with the present arrangements).

CHAPTER 4

THE PERFORMANCE MANAGEMENT OF THE HEAD

It is clear from the DfEE's consultation paper on the roles of the Head and the Governing Body, due to come into effect from September 2000, that the Government wishes governors to focus on the key objectives of the school and to be less cluttered with day-to-day matters of detail. They are invited to concentrate their efforts, energy and imagination on the strategic direction of the school and to leave the day-to-day management to the head and the staff. In other words, their principal role is to manage the performance of the head. If they can be sure of the quality of his or her performance, all will be well with the school.

In this chapter all the information already provided on the structure for the head's performance management will not be repeated. It will concentrate on the range of objectives which might be set. This is the hardest part of the job for governors and the most important in relation to their responsibility for the overall direction of the school. The official guidance from the DfEE gives examples of objectives and targets which are almost exclusively related to narrowly measurable academic targets. The challenge for governors is to make those relevant to the role of the head and also to think of other worthwhile objectives which may not be so easily measurable.

For many governors, target-setting for heads and deputies will be well established as it has been part of the STRB requirements for several years. However, in some schools target-setting is not yet firmly in place, nor will it have been as tightly prescribed as it is in the current development.

HOW MANY OBJECTIVES?

The DfEE guidance suggests between three and six objectives should be agreed. Although governors may be tempted to go for the higher figure because they may think that this is a way of making a lot of changes in the school, experience suggests that a lower number would be more effective. It is better to set a lower number of well thought-through objectives than to go for six because that is the figure mentioned. Three or possibly four would suffice and ideally these would cover:

- pupil progress (one target of this nature is mandatory)
- management activities
- professional development related to the head as an individual.

If a fourth objective is required, this might be one with a longer-term target, for example over three years, which could be monitored at the annual review and adjusted as the school develops.

WHAT OBJECTIVES SHOULD BE SET?

Pupil progress

The measurement of pupil progress is complex and Appendix 1 attempts to clarify some of the main issues. The governors face the difficulty that any appraisee can only be reviewed on objectives for which the he or she is directly responsible. It is arguable that the head can never be directly responsible for pupil progress since he or she does not teach most (or any) of the children. Yet the head clearly is responsible for creating the conditions within which children are more likely to make progress and these could be open to evaluation.

In a primary school, within an overall aim of raising the Level 4 achievement in English to 80%, the head might undertake to introduce measures which would raise the performance of boys. Evidence would come in the form of strategies introduced or encouraged and steps taken to monitor staff implementation of these strategies, as well as the statistical outcomes.

In a secondary school, improvement might be targeted at increasing the proportion of higher grades, or reducing the proportion of pupils who leave with no grades. The head would have to show what measures he or she had introduced, for example:

- earlier identification of gifted and talented pupils
- accelerated teaching and early entry
- early identification of the disaffected under-achiever *or*

- the setting-up of a mentoring system.

Governors may have to recognise that it is perfectly possible for the head to take the appropriate measures but for the results not to improve.

One pupil progress objective has to be set — governors cannot duck the issue. Their skill and sensitivity will lie in trying to identify a target which is sufficiently tight to be amenable to headteacher influence yet not too trivial. The external adviser should be able to give help.

Management activities

Many of the management activities of a head do have an indirect bearing on the way pupils progress, for example:

1. A head who is successful in raising staff morale and well being so that teacher absence rates fall will contribute to the more consistent teaching of pupils which will generally lead to better results.
2. A head who succeeds in increasing parents' participation in their children's learning will probably find that standards rise even though it will be very hard to prove a direct causal link.
3. Teaching and learning are better when pupils reach school in time so that lessons have a good start. Management measures to improve punctuality can be taken, involving pastoral staff, form-tutors, support staff, educational welfare officers. However, the direct link to improved outcomes will be difficult to prove.
4. Given what research shows about pupils doing better in school when they are motivated to attend, a head will be helping to raise standards when he or she stimulates and encourages extra-curricular activities and finds ways of making school an all-round enjoyable experience for pupils.
5. An effective manager targets scarce resources in such a way as to raise standards. He or she also knows how to link the School Development Plan to the budget. He or she takes measures to prevent scarce resources being used in unproductive ways such as having to make good pupil vandalism.
6. One of the aims of good management is to develop public relations which are so positive that parents want their children to come to the school (thereby increasing school income). One way of creating good relations with the public in general and parents in particular is to have effective measures in place to respond to complaints. Could the governors devise a target turn-round time for dealing with complaints?

7. Children are said to learn better when they work and play in an attractive school environment. A head might put in place a series of measures to redecorate the school (targeting of resources, use of volunteers) or to reduce the graffiti or litter around the school.
8. The standing of the school in the local community contributes to the number of parents who choose the school for their children, thereby increasing income which in turn leads to possible ways of enhancing the curriculum (eg, buying more books or computers) which will lead to higher standards. Local community relations depend on many factors, one of which could be positive press coverage. The head, either personally or through another member of staff, might take proactive steps to increase the number of good references to the school in the local press.
9. The accurate targeting of financial resources to learning needs is a particular skill required of effective managers. It helps to raise standards. Carrying forward large sums of money which could and should have been used for pupils is not good management. Although there will always be unanticipated factors in the course of a school budget year, a good indicator of effective management might be the closeness of match between budget and out-turn.

These examples, to which governors will be able to add from their own experience of their particular school, are chosen to illustrate the fact that what heads do does make a difference to the school but that the direct statistical and causal link between their actions and the outcomes in terms of higher standards is tenuous. In several of the areas referred to, it would not be easy to identify a significant and reliable measure. Nevertheless, over a period of years, it might well be possible for governors to choose management targets of this kind and devise measurement tools to quantify performance, for example to:

- reduce teacher absence by 5%
- increase parental attendance at consultation evenings by 10%
- increase parental attendance at curriculum information evenings by 20%
- reduce lateness in pupils by 25%
- increase pupil participation in extra-curricular activities by 20%
- reduce the proportion of the school budget spent on repairing damage caused by pupils by 25%
- put in place measures so that every complaint is acknowledged within 48 hours and a substantive answer given within 10 working days in 80% of cases.

- reduce the incidence of graffiti by 30%; to reduce litter in the school playground by 25%
- increase the number of positive reference to the school in the local press by 20%
- achieve a budget out-turn with not more than a 2% discrepancy from budget.

For any of these to be effective, the governors would need to have established in advance the baseline measures against which improvement is to be measured. This would mean planning objectives two years in advance, ie year one to devise measures and introduce monitoring, year two to confirm reliability of data, year three to set performance targets. To prevent perverse incentives (e.g. deliberate neglect by a head of these activities in the "control year" in order to improve performance in the "target year"), the governors may need to agree with the head a long list of possible indicators from which they would choose one in any particular year.

The difficult decision to be made by the governors is whether or not the indicator is sufficiently important to justify the investment of management time to explore it. There is also an issue in relation to *quantity* versus *quality*. For example, in relation to a complaints target, it might be possible for a head to achieve a rapid response rate, but if the relevance and helpfulness of the responses are poor, then there is no substantive benefit. Ultimately, it is only governors who can make a personal judgement on these qualitative factors.

Personal professional development activities

Heads, in common with all members of staff, are entitled to agree with their reviewing panel possible ways of furthering their professional development. Some may have major financial implications, others will have time pressures and may require cover to be bought in.

For example, a head may be encouraged to:

- pursue further qualifications (MBA, M.Ed., M.Phil., Ph.d, M.Sc.)
- take part in the Leadership Programme for Serving Heads (LPSH)
- if newly appointed, use HEADLAMP funding to take part in courses and conferences which fill in gaps in their previous knowledge
- seek a link to a local university or education faculty to develop an in-school action research project
- attend meetings, local conferences and national events organised by their professional associations, e.g. Secondary Heads Association (SHA), National Association for Headteachers (NAHT).

Much will depend on the future availability of funding. When training budgets have been tight, many heads have preferred to allocate funds to younger colleagues and have neglected their own development. It is the responsibility of governors to see that heads do not neglect their own development.

WHO SETS THE TARGETS?

The responsibility for agreeing the head's objectives lies with the governor panel, guided by the external adviser and in discussion with the head. There is a danger that the rest of the governing body could feel disempowered by being excluded from this process which is central to the strategic development of the school.

Some of the head's targets ought to flow from the School Development Plan into which all governors should have had an input. Through this mechanism, all governors should indirectly be involved. Some governors are worried that this might jeopardise the process for the review of the head's appraisal. If there were to be a complaint, they would not be seen as being neutral. However, it is the *appraisal of the outcomes* which is being complained about, not the targets themselves, so governors need not fear "contamination" if they are aware of the head's objectives.

THE ROLE OF THE EXTERNAL ADVISER

It is the governors who select the external adviser from a list and they will obviously choose somebody with relevant experience. The external adviser will be sent the available data on the school and will form a very preliminary view of the school's needs in terms of the targets for the head *(see Appendix 1)*.

It is suggested that the external adviser should meet separately with the head and the governors' panel prior to the joint meeting. In most cases there should be no significant disagreements between the parties concerned, but in a minority of cases it will be useful for the external adviser to have heard views independently.

The governors have an entitlement to eight hours of adviser time, free of charge, and this will be divided between the target setting phase and the review at the end of the cycle. If they feel that more time is needed, this is to be negotiated separately with the contractors. As this process is not yet in place, it is impossible to say how it will work out in detail but it seems unlikely that the eight hours could include a mid-year monitoring.

The ultimate decisions on the head's review are those of the governing body and not of the adviser.

THE LINK WITH PAY

Performance management is about raising standards and is not directly linked to higher remuneration. Any decision to move the head up the Leadership spine remains with the existing Personnel or Finance Committee which may or may not receive a recommendation from the head's review panel *(see Appendix 2)*. A decision to advance the head will depend on other budget pressures. There can be no automatic assumption that a "successful" review will lead to a pay rise. In any case, many heads are already within two points of the top of their ISR *(see Appendix 2)*.

THE SUSTAINABILITY OF THE PROCESS

Many heads have already been undergoing a target-setting and review process not unlike the one now proposed. Performance management will not come as a great shock to them. The new arrangements are more formalised and have the new ingredient of the external adviser.

Once the excitement of the initial implementation has died down, governors will have to give some thought as to how they are to sustain the momentum. Some heads stay in the same school for many years — how will the governors keep the notion of targets fresh and relevant? Many heads will reach the top of their ISR in the near future and face many more years in the same school, with an expectation of high performance and no further tangible reward.

Governors will therefore have to think of ways in which they can continue to support the head in terms of morale and challenge over an extended period of headship. This is not easy. It may be possible to plan the budget so that he or she may have a sabbatical month or term after several years in post. He or she may be encouraged to develop a teamwork approach among the leadership group so that a few weeks' absence by the head on, say further study or travel to look at schools in other countries would not have a harmful effect. It may be possible for a head to be seconded to work with the LEA or with the teacher training department of a local university or to take part in some national project, possibly in conjunction with the newly-formed National College for School Leadership. Some experienced heads could make a positive contribution to training future heads through the National Professional Qualification for Heads (NPQH) route.

The key point is that governors will have to reconcile themselves to the need to find ways other than the pay packet to keep heads alert, developing, stimulated and motivated. That is why it is so important for governors to look beyond the immediate future and have a longer-term overview of the way the school might develop and what the head's role could be.

CHAPTER 5

THE TRAINING OF GOVERNORS

The government has rightly recognised that the introduction of the Performance Management strategy makes new demands on governors and governing bodies and it has put in place a significant training programme.

Training materials have been prepared specifically for governors and a team of accredited trainers is in place to deliver training during the autumn term of 2000. The materials have been developed with a major input from experienced governor trainers. The training will mainly be delivered through the existing network of LEA governor trainers, with some independent companies being involved where the governor trainer route is not possible.

It is clearly impossible for all 350,000 governors to be trained in performance management within a few weeks and it probably is not necessary that they should be. It is nevertheless hoped that at least three governors from every school will attend the training which has been devised in three modules, each of two and a half hours duration.

MODULE 1

This is a general introduction to the principles of Performance Management and is aimed at the governing body, looking explicitly at their roles and responsibilities, especially in relation to the establishment of a school policy. The module is divided into six shorter sessions with plenty of opportunities for workshop discussion and exercises. This module will be of value to any governor who is able to attend, subject to constraints on space at the training venues.

MODULE 2

This is aimed specifically at those governors (two or three) who have been appointed by the governing body to review the head's performance. As it may be necessary for a review officer to deal with a complaint, it is advisable that an extra governor attends.

The focus is on the setting of objectives, working with the adviser and with understanding the monitoring and evaluation cycle.

Once again there are six shorter sessions with practical exercises.

MODULE 3

This is mainly about the way the head's end-of-cycle review meeting should be carried out so the same governors who attended Module 2 training need to be there.

The emphasis in this module is on the skills needed to carry out a review meeting constructively. The six shorter sessions include a chance to practise the skills by carrying out imitation review meetings.

Naturally some governors have reservations about taking part in role-play because they feel that their own skills as an actor (or lack of them) are being exposed. Participants can be reassured that the trainers are aware of this potential embarrassment and will handle participants with sensitivity.

THE VALUE OF TRAINING

The range of previous experience brought by governors to performance management will be enormous. Some will already have taken part in appraisal in their own workplace and some will have carried out appraisals of others. Paradoxically, that might make it more rather than less difficult to adapt to these school requirements.

At the other extreme, some governors may feel totally overawed at the thought of "sitting in judgement" on a person from a profession in which they have no personal experience. Their anxiety is all the greater because they know that there might be a financial implication in their judgement. "This is not what I became a governor for" is a remark already heard many times.

That is why the training will be invaluable. All will have something to learn and to contribute. As with so many other aspects of life, practice will improve performance.

PERFORMANCE MANAGEMENT CONSULTANTS

Some governing bodies may feel that they would like training on performance management within their own school for all governors, possibly with other members of staff. A team of accredited performance management consultants is in place on a regional basis and the cost of hiring them in can be covered from Standards Fund grants *(see Appendix 4)*.

Although the responsibility for carrying out the head's appraisal will lie with a small group of governors, it is important that all become familiar with what is involved so that the team can be changed from time to time. Note that teacher and other staff governors cannot be part of the head's appraisal panel or take the role of the review officer.

CHAPTER 6

CONCLUSION

As we indicated in the Introduction, the successful implementation of Performance Management in the school context represents a major challenge for all involved. In this pocket book an attempt has been made to present fairly the government's aspirations while not glossing over the difficulties.

As governors discuss these issues with heads, they will hear a number of "horror stories" about how the training was rushed, how conflicting advice has been given and about the bureaucratic workload. Without minimising these grumbles, it is important to maintain the perspective — a major potentially beneficial reform is being implemented at great speed.

Governors will benefit from attending the training and from reading this publication and many other documents that have been or will be produced. In the end, they will learn best by doing. It is only after the process has started for real that its value and its challenges will emerge.

During 2000 and 2001 governors, heads and teachers will be beset by what the government rightly calls the "challenge of change". It is essential that governors retain the overview and focus on the long-term intention which is to improve education for all our pupils.

This is why governors volunteered in the first instance to become governors and it is this which will motivate them through the difficult times which will undoubtedly lie ahead.

APPENDIX 1

MEASURING PUPIL PROGRESS

Quantifying the academic progress of pupils lies at the heart of performance management. One of the agreed objectives of all teachers and the headteacher must be related to pupil progress and one of the criteria for the Threshold assessment is specifically related to this matter *(see Chapter 3 and Appendix 5)*.

It needs to be acknowledged that many governors will be uncomfortable with the emphasis on a criterion that appears to place a higher value on measurable academic progress than on other important aspects of education such as, say, artistic development, social responsibility and environmental awareness.

In Chapter 4 it has been argued that, in setting the objectives for the headteacher, enlightened governors will try to include objectives which recognise the value of achievements other than the narrowly academic. Nevertheless, the fact remains that the overriding priority of the government's agenda is "raising standards" and this is predominantly interpreted as being academic standards as measured by tests and exams.

In this appendix we will attempt to explain how pupil progress can be quantified and presented in such a way as to be fair to teachers. What starts out as looking like a relatively simple concept is much more complex than might have been expected. This explanation is just an introduction to the topic.

MAKING PROGRESS — KNOWING MORE

It is self-evident that as children grow up they learn more and more. They learn to talk, to read with ever-increasing fluency, to make calculations of increasing complexity. They learn about the world around them, they learn how to make things, they gain a growing insight into why things happen in the way they do. This obvious "progress" does not happen in a neat sequential way or at an even pace. Children, especially younger ones, seem to make progress in spurts, followed by periods of apparent stagnation. Physical and emotional maturity, health, motivation, domestic circumstances all contribute to the pace at which a child learns.

This infinite variability of progress makes it very difficult to assert what any given child should know or be able to do at any given age. All that can be done is to devise a generalised picture of what might be expected at a given age. This means, in effect, producing a notional average performance.

This picture is created through testing, a process which has grown phenomenally in recent years. Of course, teachers have always tested children. Assessment is an integral part of the teaching process. Having taught something, you have to test children's retention and understanding of it before you can proceed to the next stage.

THE EXTENSION OF NATIONAL TESTING

Until relatively recently, the systematic testing of all young people was left until they were 16. In some areas of the country, testing at 11+ was (and is still) simply a way of determining who should have a place at a selective school. The 11+ test put pupils in rank order and the grammar school took the top 25% in order to fill the number of places available.

National testing at 16+ is organised through a number of independent Exam Boards, usually linked to a university, recently amalgamated into three large examining bodies. They are authorised to issue national certification known as the General Certificate of Secondary Education (GCSE) which replaced in 1988 the former General Certificate of Education (GCE) Ordinary Level. This is followed two years later by the GCE at Advanced Level.

In the traditional British system, the main purpose of testing was to sift out those not suitable for the next stage of education. Good results at GCE or GCSE were a pre-requisite for going into the Sixth Form and the results at Advanced Level were, indeed still are, used as an entrance filter for higher education.

Over the last decade or so, there has been a significant change in testing, both in its purpose and its scope. Although testing at 16 and older still has its function as a sieve for the next stage, testing has moved towards a system whereby a grade achieved can be linked to a positive statement of what a pupil can do. Assessment criteria have become much more specific and an attempt has been made to link a description to a grade. So although an A grade in an exam still means that the candidate has performed better than a candidate awarded a C, it is now possible to describe in more detail what a candidate at any given grade level can achieve.

The scope of testing has widened considerably. Once the National Curriculum was in place, the government of the day decided to introduce testing against the national curriculum criteria when pupils are 7 (at the end of key stage 1), 11 (at the end of key stage 2), 14 (at the end of key stage 3). Testing at KS1, although it was difficult to implement at first for teachers not used to testing in a semi-formal way, is still relatively low-key, ie it is carried out in the school using national test materials, but assessed by the teachers according to a mark-scheme provided. As pupils get older, the testing becomes more formal. At KS2, tests in English, maths and Science are taken under formal conditions and sent away to be marked. The procedure is similar at KS3.

Alongside the formal tests which are nationally set and marked, teachers have to make an individual assessment of children against the criteria for the foundation subjects, and in the other subjects at KS3. These teacher assessments have to be recorded on a pupil's record but, because they are to some extent subjective, they tend to be given less weight than the external tests.

THE PUBLICATION OF RESULTS

The testing of children gained national public prominence when the government decided to publish the aggregated results. At first it was not intended that these should be in league table form and the teaching profession was rather dismissive and professed to show no interest. In recent years, the published exam and test results of schools has been extended and the stakes raised because they have become an important criterion for the judgement of the schools by the inspection team,

OFSTED, and by the general public. Indeed, the Conservative government saw the publication of results as a mechanism for driving up standards. It was expected that parents would scrutinise the results tables and express a preference for their child to go to a high performing school. (In practice, surveys have shown that most parents prefer to choose a local school where their child will be happy rather than transport them miles to a high performing school.)

The government's argument was that schools which failed to get good results would lose pupils and thereby lose income (since 80% of a school's income is linked to pupil numbers) and this, it was alleged, would challenge or inspire them to improve.

The teaching profession has been and remains very critical of the decision to publish exam and test results in what it calls a "crude" format. The published tables show, for example, what proportion of a primary school's intake achieves Level 4 at KS2 in the three core subjects of English, Maths and Science. At 16+ they show what proportion of the year group achieves 5 higher grades (A* to C, roughly the equivalent of the former GCE O-Level pass), or 5 grade A* to G. The principal objection to the publication in this crude format is that the tables tell you nothing about the intake of the school and it is obvious that if you have a school with a selected entry, you will expect to get "better" results than a school which has a non-selective entry. Another technical weakness is that the secondary school tables record the results of pupils who are aged 15 to 16 years old. Pupils who take subjects out of their "normal" year, either because they are entered early or held back for a year, may not have their results recorded in the tables.

In a small primary school with 20 pupils in Year 6, the absence of three of the more able pupils on the day of the test could reduce the schools Level 4 percentage by 15%. The ability intake of a school varies from year to year and the smaller the school, the greater the variation in statistical terms. Given that boys under-achieve nationally relative to girls, a co-educational secondary school with more boys than girls in a particular year group will see its results deteriorate. Crude league tables reflect the entry to the school and say very little about the *quality* of the teaching.

Most recently attempts have been made to improve the league tables and these grow in complexity and scope each year. The national newspapers produce a special supplement for the results every November. For example, the secondary tables now include other indicators.

- **The number of pupils with special needs statements.** This gives a broad indication of the ability level in the school but as the number of pupils given statements depends on interpretation of criteria and the school having the money implement the statement, it is not a reliable indicator of the school's ability intake.
- **Unauthorised absence — percentage of half days missed.** Again this may give a broad indication of the kind of catchment area served by the school but the interpretation of "authorised" and "unauthorised" is not consistent across schools.
- **The average pupil score.** This is arrived at by dividing the total points scored by the pupils (A* = 8, A = 7, B = 6, etc) and dividing by the number of pupils in the year group. In some ways this is a better measure than the five higher grade hurdle because it is an encouragement to pupils and teachers to raise performance at all levels but it too has a technical weakness. Some schools have a policy of not entering pupils for subjects at which they might get a low grade. Others deliberately enter pupils for as many subjects as possible. The costs of examination entries, although only marginal in the whole of a school's budget, might influence the school's entry policy. All these factors could distort the average pupil score. A fairer measure would be to take the best seven or eight subjects of all pupils and calculate the average of that performance.

In the league tables for both primary and secondary schools, comparative scores in recent years are provided to show "improvement". This seems a good idea but percentage changes are vulnerable to the performance of very few pupils in smaller schools. In primary schools, the percentage gaining Level 4 in English, maths and Science are added together to provide the school improvement measure.

VALUE-ADDED MEASURE

In order to compare the performance of schools and teachers equitably, it is clearly necessary to have a better picture of the ability level and socio-economic circumstances of the pupils in the school. By measuring all the children in the country, it is possible to create an expected level of absolute progress against which the progress of any individual child can be measured. In this way it is possible to quantify the extra progress (or lack of it) in a pupil's progress compared with children of the same ability. This is what is called the "value-added" factor. For any individual pupil, or for a class or a school if you add individual scores together, it could be a positive or a negative figure.

For example, all the children in the country take a maths test; It is marked out of 100 and the average score is 50. At a later date, they all take another maths test and this time the average score is 52. The difference in the two scores is NOT a value-added factor. It simply means that the pupils found the second test slightly easier. An average pupil who scored 50 in the first test might be expected to score 52 in the second test if he has made the expected progress. If he has scored 63, for example, he has a positive value-added score of 11. If he has scored 41, he has a negative value-added score of 11.

As the design of tests is never perfect, it is recognised that minor variations are not significant. Test designers usually state at what level of variation any score can said to be significant.

The value-added approach is broadly welcomed by teachers and heads as giving a fairer reflection of the work done by schools. It enables LEAs and OFSTED to produce "benchmark data" which show how well a school has done relative to schools in similar circumstances and with similar intakes across an LEA and across the nation. This information is sent to schools in their PANDA (Performance and Assessment Report) and it is essential that governors who are involved in setting objectives have a detailed look at this data. It includes information on:

- the basic characteristics of the school
- the school context
- inspection judgements
- school attendance
- attainment — broad overview
- attainment at relevant key stages in comparison with national averages.

Schools receive an "Autumn Package" which enables them to compare themselves with schools of similar background and to study the extent to which they are performing above or below the levels expected by virtue of the background of the pupils. Free school meals rates are used as a proxy indicator for background and although this may be broadly acceptable as an indicator of social disadvantage, many assessment specialists do not accept them as an accurate indicator of educational disadvantage. The Autumn Package also shows progress from one key stage to another, eg what might pupils be expected to score at KS3 in the light of their KS2 scores. As an indicator of prior achievement, that might seem to be more convincing were it not for the fact that many teachers have reservations about the relationship between levels at the different key stages. For example, some pupils coming into a secondary school with a Level 5 in English at KS2 seem not to progress to a higher level at KS3. This is because the tests are different and the levels do not show continuity across the phases.

WINNERS AND LOSERS

The essence of the value-added approach is that it sets a benchmark figure for average progress. This obviously means that half are below and half above average! The criterion for pupil progress in the Threshold Assessment is that teachers should provide evidence that their pupils have made progress "as good or better than similar pupils nationally" *(see Chapter 3 and Appendix 5).*

If this is interpreted narrowly, half the teachers in the country will not be able to meet this criterion. Similarly, if the same criterion is applied to the head's objective for the whole school, it can only be achieved by half of the nation's heads, however brilliant they may be in raising standards.

The effect of using the value-added approach is to increase the challenge for schools each year. This is no doubt the reason why the government wants to adopt it as it is a powerful force for raising standards. As a mechanism for judging the performance of an individual teacher or head, it has its limitations and governors should not use this criterion in a narrow and mechanistic way when evaluating the head's objectives. Nor should a head or team leader when evaluating the performance of an individual teachers against targets.

Clearly a teacher will probably be doing a pretty good job if his or her pupils approximate to the national value-added pattern. A small negative value-added score could not be used as a reason for not approving a threshold application, nor could a whole-school negative score be used as a criticism of a head. Much will depend on what governors and heads judge to be "small".

If a teacher or a school continues to have a significant negative value-added score over several years, that might clearly be a cause for concern.

NOT ALL SUBJECTS ARE EQUALLY DIFFICULT

All governors will have their own memories of struggling with certain subjects at school. Rarely does an individual pupil get exactly the same grade in all subjects across the range, say, at GCSE. This is understandable since we all have different strengths, talents and weaknesses but it is made more complicated by the fact that it is easier to get high grades in some subjects than others.

When governors look at the school's results after the GCSE results have been published, they instinctively tend to look at the proportion of higher grades achieved in order to judge the performance of that department. What governors do not find it easy to appreciate is that it is more difficult to get higher grades in some subjects than others. The relative difficulty of subjects is revealed each year in the "residual" which an LEA supplies to schools early in the Autumn term. The table of residuals shows how pupils in any given school have performed in their various subjects and highlights which subjects have contributed most to the school's overall performance and which least. Every subject has a positive or negative residual. When a subject has +0.50 as its residual, that means that all the pupils who took that subject scored, on average, half a grade higher than the pupils as a whole scored in all the other subjects. Conversely, the pupils taking a subject with a negative residual have performed less well. However, before jumping to conclusions about the performance of the various departments in the school, it is important for governors to read across to see what the residuals are for all the pupils in the LEA area and across the whole of England. This information is usually provided in tabular form which looks like the example below.

Subject description	A **Number of pupils entered**	B **School subject residual**	C **LEA area subject residual**	D **England subject residual**
Science, double award	150	0.09	0.07	0.05
Mathematics	146	-0.38	-0.25	-0.26
CDT: Design & Communication	32	-0.18	-0.54	-0.42
CDT: Design & Realisation	47	-0.61	-0.04	0.00

HE: Food	17	-0.63	0.19	0.09
Art and Design	30	0.38	1.20	0.70
Geography	94	0.77	-0.07	-0.09
History	33	-0.65	-0.15	-0.20
Religious Studies	31	0.31	0.03	-0.27
English	154	-0.11	0.13	0.22
English Literature	140	-0.17	0.08	0.17
Drama	72	0.88	0.82	0.69
French	66	-0.28	-0.43	-0.29
German	77	-0.09	-0.45	-0.30
Music	14	0.81	0.44	0.01

The first thing to remember when looking at such a table is that subjects with a small number of pupils entering for the exam (column A) cannot fairly be compared with a large entry subject. This is because a small entry subject may be highly selective in the school, i.e. only those keenest on the subject and most able at it are entered. In the above table, this is clearly the case with music. Looking at the above table column B, it appears clear that the Drama department has done well but when you look across to column C , it is clear that this result is in line with what all pupils have done throughout the LEA area. Looking across to column D, this confirms that across the country, pupils taking that subject have achieved higher grades. The more accurate interpretation of the school's result in drama is that the pupils have performed broadly according to national norms.

On the other hand, pupils taking German who appear to have done badly because they have a negative residual, have in fact done quite well relative to the performance in that subject by pupils in other schools. This might suggest that the teachers of that subject have added value to the performance of their pupils. In the above school, most subjects are performing close to national expectations but there is a problem with english, history and CDT design and realisation, whereas geography, german and religious studies are doing well.

The position is further complicated by the difference in performance between boys and girls. Girls find some subjects easier than boys and, across the country, have a higher residual. Separate tables are produced by gender and it is worth looking at these. Depending on which optional subjects pupils decide to take, a mixed school with a year group with more boys than girls may find its overall performance drops even though the teachers have been working just as hard as they did in previous years when results were "better" because there was a more even balance of girls and boys in the cohort.

For schools with A-Level pupils, sophisticated data are available if the school subscribes to ALIS (A-Level Information System) run by researchers at Durham University. This shows the difficulty in obtaining high grades at A-Level compared to a pupil's overall score at GCSE. Subjects which are the most difficult are physics and french.

Whether or not there should be this difference of difficulty in the grading of subjects is a matter of debate among test specialists. Some argue on equity grounds that the grades for each subject should be adjusted to even out the difficulty factor. Others argue that the examiners must try to maintain standards year on year by judging the performance of candidates according to agreed criteria. This, it is argued, maintains the "gold standard" of A-Level. Whatever the rights and wrongs of this argument, the important point for governors to retain is that you cannot make snap judgements on the achievement of departments by looking simply at the examination results. Nor can you judge an individual teacher or the school as a whole without an awareness of national patterns and trends.

CHILDREN WITH SPECIAL EDUCATIONAL NEEDS

If national tables have their limitations for mainstream children, they are even less helpful for children with special educational needs (SEN). Progress in many cases will be measured against Individual Education Plans (IEPs). A DfEE booklet *Supporting the Target Setting Process* shows how criteria can be established for SEN pupils in the domains of language, literacy, mathematics and personal/social development. SEN teachers have developed particular expertise in setting targets and measuring progress.

RECOMMENDED READING

- *Monitoring Education: Indicators, Quality and effectiveness,* Carol Taylor Fitz-Gibbon, Cassell

APPENDIX 2

THE NEW PAY STRUCTURE

From September 2000, the government has introduced a new pay structure for teachers which fits in with the performance management policy. Instead of a single 17 point spine for all teachers, into which experience, responsibility points and recruitment allowances were jumbled, there is now a much clearer structure.

THE BASIC SPINE

The **basic spine** has 9 points, as follows:

Spine point	£ per annum
1	15,141
2	16,050
3	16,923
4	17,844
5	18,906
6	20,046
7	21,249
8	22,524
9	23,958

As before, teachers start on point 1 or 2 according to qualifications. They can also be placed higher up the spine if they have relevant experience outside teaching. There are no specific guidelines for governors appointing new staff with previous non-teaching experience. Governors have to decide whether or not the previous experience will contribute significantly to the performance of the teacher's duties. Some relevant bodies allow one experience point for every three years of other relevant experience, up to a maximum of three. These points are discretionary but once allocated cannot be removed. Points allocated by a previous school must be honoured if the teacher moves to a new school.

The expectation is that a teacher will move up the spine on an annual incremental basis. The procedures for evaluating performance will be more rigorous as the performance management regime comes into effect. A point may be withheld for unsatisfactory performance, but it is not recommended that Governors should take this measure unless the teacher has already been subject to disciplinary or competence proceedings. If a point is withheld and the teacher subsequently makes a significant improvement, the incremental point can be restored. An innovation from 2000 is that exceptionally good performance can be rewarded with a double increment.

The basic pay spine is extended into an **upper pay range**, as follows:

Spine point	£ per annum
1	25,959
2	26,919
3	27,915
4	28,947
5	30,018

Advancement through the upper pay range is not incremental. It will be subject to appraisal which will be increasingly rigorous. IThe details of further advancement have not yet been specified, but there will be further guidance before the first candidates become eligible in 2002.

ADDITIONAL ALLOWANCES

Points which could previously be allocated for responsibilities, recruitment and retention and special needs, have been replaced as follows:

	£ per annum
Management 1	1,485
Management 2	3,000
Management 3	5,151
Management 4	7,092
Management 5	9,573
Recruitment and retention 1	909

Recruitment and retention 2	1,782
Recruitment and retention 3	2,703
Recruitment and retention 4	3,765
Special needs 1	1,485
Special needs 2	3,000

Management allowances

These are to be awarded for clearly defined and substantial management tasks undertaken in addition to normal professional duties. The allowances have the same cash value as the gap between the previous point 9 and points 10 to 14. The former half-points have disappeared. Management allowances can be awarded on a temporary basis so this restores some flexibility for headteachers and governors who feel that the management allowances are too crude and large.

Recruitment and retention allowances

These may be used as in the former system to attract teachers in shortage subjects or to hold on to a teacher who might otherwise leave. The first two allowances may be awarded to all teachers and the third allowance in schools in inner London and in schools under special measures. The fourth allowance is only available for schools in special measures in Inner London.

Special needs allowances

These are distributed in the same way as in the former system: the first one is mandatory for all teachers in special schools and the second point can be awarded where the relevant body judges that the teacher's experience or qualifications enhance the work being undertaken.

THE LEADERSHIP SPINE

The pay spines for heads and deputies are re-designated as the **Leadership Spine** and become the structure for senior teachers. A new title of assistant head has been coined for those who are placed on the Leadership spine (mainly those who were formerly receiving 5 responsibility points for whole school responsibilities).

The Leadership spine from September 2000 is as follows:

APPENDIX 2

Spine point (September 2000)	Salary (£pa)
L1	28,446
L2	29,157
L3	29,886
L4	30,633
L5	31,398
L6	32,184
L7	32,988
L8	33,813
L9	34,659
L10	35,526
L11	36,408
L12	37,314
L13	38,244
L14	39,198
L15	40,173
L16	41,172
L17	42,195
L18	43,251
L19	44,322
L20	45,423
L21	46,548
L22	47,703
L23	48,885
L24	50,097
L25	51,339
L26	52,611
L27	53,906
L28	55,254
L29	56,625
L30	58,029
L31	59,469
L32	60,945
L33	62,457
L34	64,005
L35	65,592
L36	67,218
L37	68,899
L38	70,593
L39	72,312
L40	74,121
L41	75,972

PLACING HEADS ON THE LEADERSHIP SPINE

Heads in post will have had their salary point fixed in 1999 on the basis of the 1999 arrangements which divided schools into eight groups, based on a unit total calculation as follows:

Key Stage	Units per pupil	Total Unit Score	School Group
Prestage 1, 1 and 2	7	up to 1,000	1
3	9	1001 to 2,200	2
4	11	2,201 to 3,500	3
5	13	3,501 to 5,000	4
		5,001 to 7,500	5
		7,501 to 11,000	6
		11,001 to 17,000	7
		17,001 and above	8

The range of spine points in each group is as follows:

Group	Spine points from September 2000
Group 1	L6–L16
Group 2	L8–L19
Group 3	L11–L22
Group 4	L14–L25
Group 5	L18–L29
Group 6	L21–L33
Group 7	L24–L37
Group 8	L28–L41

Using these ranges as a guide, the Governors decide the Individual School Range (ISR) for the school, bearing in mind any special circumstances, socio-economic pressures, recruitment difficulties, local benchmarking, etc. The ISR has a seven point range and this range will be fixed according to where the school fits into the group size. New Heads are placed at the bottom of the range, Heads appointed before 1999 are placed to allow at least two further points for progression. In exceptional circumstances the range may be extended two points above the top of the group size.

HEAD TEACHERS OF SPECIAL SCHOOLS

The formula to determine a school's group is more complex than for mainstream schools as it attempts to take into account not only the number of pupils on roll, but the severity of need as reflected in the number of teachers employed. To calculate the unit total for a school and therefore place it into a group, the proposed formula uses the key stage weighted pupil unit total calculated as for mainstream schools (with three points added for each statemented pupil). This is then multiplied by a "modifier" which is determined buy the staff-pupil ratio. The resulting total assigns the school to a group, as with mainstream schools, except that the lowest group for any special school is group 2.

The modifier is calculated by taking the full-time equivalent (FTE) of teaching staff multiplied by 2 added to the full-time equivalent of other staff, producing a weighted total FTE staff. This figure is divided by the number of pupils and multiplied by 100, producing a staff-pupil ratio as a percentage figure. The table of modifiers is as follows:

Staff/Pupil ratio (%)	**Modifier**
1–20	1
21–35	2
36–50	3

THE CREATION OF THE NEW LEADERSHIP GROUP

From September 2000, teachers with strategic whole school responsibilities may become members of the leadership group and are paid on the leadership spine (LS). The assimilation process is that such teachers move across from their present salary to a point on the leadership spine which gives them a pay rise of at least £2001, thus putting them in an equal position with colleagues who do cross the threshold. This point on the LS becomes the bottom point on their five point Individual Salary Range (ISR). Teachers moving on to the Leadership spine are no longer subject to the 1,265 hours contractual limitation which affects classroom teachers.

The position of the deputy is that his or her ISR also consists of 5 points, the top one of which is at least one point below the ISR of the head. The assistant head's ISR may overlap with that of the deputy/deputies, but the bottom point of a deputy head's ISR must be at least one point above that of an assistant head.

Further progression up the ISR for deputies and assistant heads is subject to the performance management review policy.

APPENDIX 3

THE PERFORMANCE MANAGEMENT MODEL POLICY

In order to simplify matters for schools, the DfEE has published a model policy. This gives governors and heads a flying start but does not absolve them from consulting with staff on certain issues. Although there are many ways in which all schools are similar, there are also differences which should be reflected in the school's policy.

The structure of the model policy is reprinted below. The extracts printed in ordinary typeface are the DfEE recommendations; those printed in **bold** are mandatory and those printed in *[italic with square brackets]* are comments from the author of this pocket book, particularly highlighting issues which governors might like to consider.

1. INTRODUCTION

In this school we are committed to performance management to develop all staff and improve teaching and to raise standards of achievement for All children. To do this we shall be introducing a Performance Management Policy based on the Performance Management system which comes into statutory force from September 2000. This policy covers all teachers except teachers on contracts of less than one year and those in their induction year. All teachers have been consulted in developing this policy. It sets a framework for all staff to agree and review priorities and objectives within the context of the school's development plan and their own professional needs.

[There will be some staff who are unwilling to sign up, as it were, to the opening statement. They might well believe that they have already spent many years improving teaching and raising standards without the paraphernalia of PM. Given that the implementation of the policy is mandatory, it is not worth spending a long time on this.]

[Key issues for governors to raise with head are, how exactly are staff to be consulted? Will this be only at the PM Inset days, or will staff have a chance to discuss the implications in smaller groups, e.g. in faculty or key stage teams? In particular, to what extent have the potential team leaders been consulted since they are going to be in the hot seats? Is there to be an appeals procedure so that a member of staff can request a change of team leader prior to the first stage of the process?]

2. RATIONALE

Performance management means a shared commitment to high performance. It helps to focus attention on more effective teaching and monitoring to raise the quality of teaching and to benefit pupils, teachers and the school. It means providing appropriate and effective personal training and development to ensure job satisfaction, a high level of expertise and progression of staff in their chosen profession.

We want to improve school performance by developing the effectiveness of teachers, both as individuals and as teams. The evidence is that standards rise when school and individual teachers are clear about what they expect pupils to achieve. That is why performance management is important.

We will implement our performance management arrangements on the basis of:

(i) Fairness. We all need to be aware of the potential for unconscious discrimination and to avoid assumptions about individuals based on stereotypes, *and*

(ii) Equal Opportunity. All teachers should be encouraged and supported to achieve their potential through agreeing objectives, undertaking development and having their performance assessed.

[These ideas could be expressed more concisely and the sentences in the first paragraph could be broken into shorter ones for greater clarity and impact.]

[Governors may want to ask precisely what evidence there is to support the assertion of the second sentence in the second paragraph. Experienced heads may wish to rephrase this sentence by adding "and make these expectations

clear to pupils and parents". Most teachers are already clear in their own minds about what they expect but do not communicate these expectations clearly to pupils.]

[As there is clearly potential for conscious as well as unconscious discrimination, it may be better to omit the adjective.]

3. ROLES

Performance management is a shared responsibility. The governing body has a strategic role in agreeing the school's performance management policy, ensuring that the performance of teachers at the school is regularly reviewed and for monitoring the Performance Management process. The headteacher is responsible for implementing the school's performance management policy and ensuring that the performance management reviews take place. Performance management involves both the team leader and the teacher working together to ensure that objectives are discussed and agreed; regular and objective feedback is given; adequate coaching, training and development is provided and that the performance review takes place. An external adviser will provide advice to the governing body's representatives on the setting of performance objectives for the head and will support them in reviewing performance at the end of the review cycle. A more detailed breakdown of statutory roles and responsibilities is included in the summary of the Regulations at Annex A.

[The idea expressed in the first sentence is an important one and worthy of further discussion at staff consultations. There is a widespread feeling that PM is something inflicted on teachers by the head. If teachers do not cooperate sensibly and positively with whoever is their team leader, the process will become conflictual and will not achieve the ambitious aspirations enunciated in sections 1 and 2 of the policy.]

[How the feedback of an individual on the work of another individual can ever be truly "objective" is debatable. The intention is probably that there should be some statistical component rather than just an expression of personal opinion.]

[The Annex referred to is probably the most significant part of the document since it specifies who does what and when. It will need careful adaptation to the particular needs of each school.]

ANNEX A

The Governing Body

- must determine the procedures for the performance review of school teachers at the school. (It is proposed that the **School Government Regulations 1999**(SI No. 2242) will make it a statutory requirement that these should be embodied in a school performance management policy, developed after consultation with staff and reviewed annually.)

[The sentence in brackets will be irrelevant since most governing bodies will not get round to setting up the policy until after it has become statutory. It will however be important for the governors to establish how the annual review of the policy will take place. Will it be consist of a presentation on the matter to the full governors by the teacher governors? Will it be handled by the Personnel Committee? Will the chair of governors meet the whole staff, or an elected group of the staff, or the team leaders, or will it be left to the head to carry out the review?]

Is responsible for:

- securing that the performance of teachers is reviewed in accordance with the Regulations.

[This suggests that the head must give a regular report on the process to the Personnel Committee.]

- appointing an accredited external adviser from an approved list.

[The governors will want to be sure that the external adviser they appoint has experience relevant to the particular school. NB it is the governors who choose the adviser, not the head.]

- deciding on the exact timing of the performance review cycle for the headteacher.

[Late November or early December seems to be the most appropriate moment. The benchmark data will have been received, the budget-creation process will not yet have started in detail, end-of-term exhaustion will not have struck. If there are to be radically different objectives for the succeeding year, it will be difficult to implement them at that point in the year as the curriculum, staffing and timetable will be set. This is why it is more likely that, once the process is established, objectives will more usefully be set for two or three years down the line.]

- carrying out the performance review of the headteacher. In so doing it appoints two or three governors to carry out the performance review. At Church schools, at least one representative should be a foundation governor. Representatives should not include teachers or other members of the staff at the school.

[It will be interesting to see whether there will be a rush of volunteers to undertake this task. Initial reactions suggest that there may be difficulties in some primary schools with small governing bodies where most of those on it are members of staff (either directly elected or as parent governors). "Two or three" is a key issue. If it were to come to a recommendation on whether or not the head should move up the leadership spine, a panel of two might be split. Three members seems more sensible, but it has to be remembered that there must be a separate shadow panel in the event of a complaint. Another key issue is the role of the chair of governors: as the person who works most closely with the head, he/she is an obvious choice for membership of the panel. On the other hand, the working relationship might be too close for an objective appraisal.]

- ensuring that, in the first performance review cycle, headteacher objectives are set and recorded by 31 December 2000 and teacher objectives by the end of February 2001
- appointing one or more review officers where a complaint is made by the headteacher about his or her performance review and the chair of governors has been involved in the performance review.

The chair of governors

The chair of governors:

- is the review officer for complaints from the headteacher where the chair has not been involved in the performance review, and for teachers where the headteacher is the team leader

[The chair of governors clearly has to think through what his or her role is going to be since he or she could become very involved in the process if things go badly wrong. Note that, unlike the previous arrangements where the governors set objectives for the deputy head(s), deputy heads and assistant heads (see Appendix 2) are to be appraised by the headteacher.]

- must provide any review officer or new reviewer with a copy of the performance review statement and with the objectives relating to that statement.
- pass the training and development annex of the head's performance review statement to the person responsible for training and development in the school

[It is not yet clear how much money is going to be available for the training and development needs emerging from the review process. In the past many heads have been reluctant to spend any or much of the very small training budget on

themselves. This is particularly the case in small schools where the head is also the person responsible for staff training and development. The Chair of Governors should insist that, where a clear need has been identified, the head should receive the relevant training.]

- must provide a copy of the head's appraisal statement to the CEO, or a designated officer, where the school does not have a delegated budget.

Governors

The governors responsible for reviewing the performance of the headteacher must:

- seek advice from the appointed external adviser when setting objectives and reviewing the performance of the headteacher
- meet with the headteacher and adviser at the start of the performance review cycle to plan and prepare for the performance review, and set and record headteacher objectives relating to school leadership and management and pupil progress

[It is suggested that, initially, the external adviser might meet separately with the governors panel and with the headteacher. In the training sessions for governors, there has been some debate about which of those two meetings should come first but in the end it will not make much difference. The external adviser, who will probably be an experienced head (or have relevant experience) and will have been trained for the purpose, will be able to pick up any differences of opinion between governors and head and be sensitive to any tensions in the relationship. Where such tensions exist, the external adviser will be careful to bring a calm and objective external perspective to the situation.]

- meet with the headteacher and adviser at the end of the performance review cycle to review the head's performance and identify achievements, including assessment of achievement against objectives, and to discuss and identify professional needs/activities
- write a performance review statement and give a copy to the headteacher within 10 days of the review meeting, and allow 10 days for the headteacher to add written comments
- provide the headteacher and chair of the governing body with a copy of the headteacher's performance review statement

[These requirements make it clear why the governors need to attend the training which is to be provided (see Chapter 5). Although one does not want to assume that there will be difficulties, it is apparent that differences of opinion between the head and governors, and even between the governors, could emerge. The governors themselves have to write the review statement and cannot rely on the

services of the clerk to the governors in this matter. Concern has been expressed about the creation of a two tier governing body, i.e. the "important and influential" ones being on the review panel. There is no reason why other members of the governing body should not suggest to the panel matters they would like to see raised at the initial objective-setting meeting. They could also be informed of the objectives which have been set for the head. Non-panel members would not be involved in assessing the performance against the objectives because they would need to keep themselves "uncontaminated" in case they are called upon in the event of a complaint by the headteacher.]

- on request, provide a copy of the headteacher's statement to those governors who are responsible for taking decisions in relation to promotion and pay, who should take account of it when making such decisions.

The interpretation of this clause may cause some difficulty and require the governing body to rethink its committee structure. Much depends on the current arrangements: who now takes decisions on promotion and pay? Is it the Finance Committee, is it the Personnel Committee, or a sub-group of one or other? In the first year, when headteacher promotion on the basis of performance will be directly funded by central government (see Appendix 5), there may be no great difficulty in reaching a decision. The really difficult decisions will come in subsequent years when the pressure from the review panel for a promotion for the head has to be set against other pressures, e.g. books and equipment for the pupils. What is clear is that a positive assessment, i.e. the head has achieved all the objectives set, challenging as they were, will not automatically bring about a pay enhancement. The head's ISR (see Appendix 2) has an upper limit in any case so a head who remains in post in the same school will have to get used to meeting the objectives without extra financial reward.

The Headteacher

The headteacher:

- as proposed, will be responsible under the **School Government Regulations 1999** (SI No. 2242) for overseeing the implementation of the school's performance management policy and may be asked by the governing body to draft the policy for consultation with staff and agreement by the government body.

[The wording is slightly surprising in that it suggests ("may be asked") that a governing body may take it on itself to produce the draft. The most practical way forward is for the governors to set up a small working party which will receive a first draft from the head, set in place consultation procedures with the

staff, revise the draft in the light of consultation, put the revised draft to the full governing body, revise it again in the light of comments from the full governing body and then confirm it as the school's policy.]

The headteacher is responsible for:

- appointing an appropriate team leader for each teacher, to carry out their performance review

[This is likely to be one of the most sensitive aspects of the whole process. The team leader must obviously be well placed to understand the work of the teacher being appraised, yet too close a relationship may make it impossible to be objective. A pre-existing poor relationship between teacher and potential team leader cannot be resolved by imposition. The head will need to consider whether or not a teacher has a right of appeal against a particular nomination. Ultimately, the head will have to decide.]

- deciding on the exact timing of the performance review cycle for teachers
- deciding on the exact length of the first performance review cycle for teachers

[There is no simple answer on these points. Much will depend on the cycle of activities within the particular school. Common sense suggests that the cycle for all the teachers might be completed before the head's review meeting since the successful completion of the review cycle may well be one of the head's objectives. Care must be taken to avoid overloading team leaders. It is probable that the process will take longer than originally anticipated.]

- providing a copy of the teacher's review statement to any review officer, including the objectives relevant to that statement
- ensuring that current objectives are made available to a teacher's new team leader, if there is a change of reviewer.

[The turnover of staff is likely to be one of the disruptive factors in the implementation of this policy. If a team leader leaves mid-cycle, as may well happen if the cycle is not co-terminous with the school year, it will be a matter for careful consideration as to whether the incoming member of staff, for example, a new key stage co-ordinator, head of department/faculty, deputy head, picks up the appraisees of the previous team leader or whether they are re-allocated to an existing member of staff who will have a closer knowledge of their work. It makes sense therefore that careful notes of mid-year monitoring are kept so that an incoming team leader will have a good information base on which to draw.]

The headteacher must:

- provide an annual report on performance management in the school to the governing body. It should contain a report on the operation of performance management in the school, the effectiveness of the school's performance management procedures and the training and development needs of the teachers

- provide whoever is responsible for planning and coordinating teachers' training and development in the school with a copy of the part of the performance review statement that relates to training and development

[As stated above, it is not yet clear whether every school will receive a guaranteed INSET budget related to the number of teachers or whether there will be a ring-fenced entitlement for every individual teacher, or whether a notional sum will be included in the schools general revenue budget. Since it is unlikely that there will be enough money to meet every identified need, the governors may well have to be involved in devising a strategic policy for the allocation of funds.]

- keep teachers' performance review statements secured on file until at least three years after the next performance statement has been finalised

[It is not yet clear to what extent performance reviews will be used or quoted in job applications and references. This may be an area for local agreement.]

- review complaints by teachers about their review statement, where they are not the team leader

[In a large school, this clause could give the head a lot of work, which suggests that his or her own personal allocation of appraisees should not be too great.]

- pass a copy of the performance review statement to those teachers for whom they are team leader
- on request, provide a copy of the performance review statement to those governors who are responsible for taking decisions in relation to promotion and pay, who should take account of this when making such decisions

[It is not clear from this wording who is making the request. Is it the governors who request this information or is it the teacher who requests that it should be passed to the relevant governors? There is no direct link between the statement and pay except in the case of teachers not on point 9 of the main scale who may be eligible for a "double jump" or those who are on the upper pay spine and wish to progress further. The criteria for advancement on the upper pay spine are not yet known, nor is it clear how the cost implications of any internal decisions by the governors will be adequately covered by the funding distribution mechanism.]

- on request, pass a copy of the performance review statement to a teacher's team leader.

[A strange clause, given that it is the team leader who has written the statement in the first place. The implication is that the team leader can ask to keep copies for future reference. Given that the team leader will, in most cases, continue as a team leader for the subsequent year, it would seem self-evident that he or she will want to keep a copy of the statement they have written.]

The headteacher as a jobholder must:

- meet with the appointed reviewers and external adviser to agree objectives at the start of the performance review cycle
- meet with the appointed reviewers and external adviser to review performance at the end of the performance review cycle, including achievement against objectives.

[Could be shortened into one sentence.]

The headteacher as a jobholder may:

- add written comments to the record of objectives set by his or her reviewers
- add written comments to the performance review statement or lodge an appeal against the performance review statement, within 10 days of receipt from the governors.

[It will be interesting to see how frequently complaints will be lodged. A complaint and the subsequent re-review, leading possibly to a grudging acceptance by the head, could sour relations for the forthcoming year(s). This is the risk factor in the whole policy and only time will tell whether this will become a serious cause of friction and grievance.]

The team leader

The team leader must:

- meet with each of the teachers for whom they will be the reviewer before or at the start of the performance review cycle to plan and prepare for performance review and discuss setting objectives
- record objectives in writing and allow the job holder to add written comments if they wish. Teacher objectives must include those relating to developing and improving a teacher's professional practice and pupil progress

[This is clearly the heart of the whole process. The success or failure of performance management will depend on the quality of the work at this level. The training of team leaders is a major challenge for the head and senior staff. Team leaders should also be encouraged to share good ideas among themselves. Objectives must be realistic yet challenging. Good background data will be

essential and this will be increasingly refined over the coming years. It will also be important to decide whether other criteria, less number-driven, can be agreed.]

- monitor performance against these objectives throughout the year, and observe the teacher teaching in the classroom at least once during the review cycle

[A single observation is the minimum statutory requirement and is probably less than many team leaders already do as a matter of course in their normal work as curriculum coordinator or head of department. Some of the objectives will not be amenable to measurement during the year as they will relate to national test or public examination outcomes later in the cycle. The team leader will also want to look at lesson planning notes, record of marks and samples of pupils' work.]

[The model policy includes an Annex C with a sample lesson observation form, assessment grid and guidance. This is not reproduced here because it goes into a level of detail which is not relevant to governors. Notes from these observations will be relevant to the eventual Threshold application of those teachers not yet eligible (see Chapter 3 for details).]

- consult the reviewee before obtaining oral or written information from others relating to the teacher's performance

[Some secondary school teachers may well want to include as one of their objectives their performance as a tutor or as a person with a pastoral responsibility. Their reviewer may be a head of department so evidence from a senior pastoral colleague will be relevant. The important point to note is that, in the interests of equity and openness, the appraisee should know from whom information is being sought.]

- meet with the teacher at the end of the performance review cycle to review performance and identify achievements, including assessment of achievement against objectives, and to discuss and identify professional development needs/activities.
- write performance review statement and give a copy to the reviewee within 10 days of the final performance review meeting and allow 10 days for the jobholder to add written comments
- pass the completed performance review statement to the headteacher.

[Most teachers are by now familiar with the conditions which are essential for an effective meeting of this kind. The setting must be calm and free from interruption. The team leader must put the appraisee at their ease; positive statements of achievement must not be taken for granted but spelt out; remarks, especially any which may be construed as a criticism, must be supported by clear evidence; everything which the reviewer intends to put in the written

statement must have been covered in the meeting; the discussion must be frank but positive and should end with a clear indication of what can be done to help the teacher, however well they have done, to do even better in future. In the vast majority of cases, the meeting will go well; it is the small minority where there are grounds for criticism which may cause difficulty. There may be a need for in-service training for team leaders on how to handle a difficult review meeting as it requires skills and a sensitivity which may not come easily to all team leaders, even those who are themselves very successful teachers. There will also be the problem of some team leaders having themselves received a less than glowing statement from their team leader and who may be subconsciously inclined to "take it out" on their appraisees. This may suggest that the timing of the process should require team leaders to carry out their reviews of teachers before they are themselves appraised.]

The jobholder (school teachers who are not headteachers)

The jobholder must:

- meet with their team leader before or at the start of the performance review cycle to discuss setting objectives
- either agree objectives or add written comments to the objectives recorded by the team leader
- meet with the team leader at the end of the performance review cycle to review performance and identify achievements, including assessment of achievement against objectives, and to discuss and identify professional development needs/activities
- may add comments to the performance review statement or complain about their performance review statement within 10 days of receipt from the team leader.

[Annex C concludes by repeating the guidance on the review cycle and clarifying that if a teacher moves to new school, they move on to the new school review cycle even if that means that their review period is less than a year. It also specifies that if, after a complaint, a new whole or partial review is ordered, it must be carried out within 15 days of the complaint being made.]

4. RESPONSIBILITY FOR REVIEWS

We have carefully considered the practical arrangements for performance management in the school. We have appointed two governors to carry out the head's performance management review. The head has decided who shall act as team leader for each teacher on the basis of responsibility for learning in the school, a judgement about who has the best overview of the teacher's work and the ability to provide support to staff. In doing this, the head has delegated responsibility to an appropriate team leader to ensure that each reviewer is responsible for a limited number of reviews. In some cases this is the head. Good practice shows that reviewers do not have more than 6 reviewees. We have decided that we will limit the number of reviewees to 4.

[Think carefully before appointing only two governors.]

5. TIMING OF REVIEWS

The one year performance management cycle links with our planning for school management and target-setting. **The Governing Body needs to ensure that objectives have been agreed or set for the head by the end of December 2000 and for all other teaching staff by the end of February, 2001.**

Our timetable is shown below:

(a) **Objectives set in the Autumn term 2000/Spring Term 2001**

These will inform and support our school management policies for the financial and academic years 2001/2002 and 2002/2003. We will take account of professional development objectives in setting the school's overall priorities for staff development.

[The words in bold are statutory. The fact that the financial and academic years are not the same does not help with the level of planning implied in this statement.]

(b) **Monitoring and Feedback**

This section explains the school's arrangements for review, including at least one classroom observation for each teacher.

[Review is used in this section slightly confusingly to refer to the monitoring process during the year. It would be clearer to call this "monitoring" and keep the word "review" for the formal review at the end of the cycle.]

(c) Formal Reviews Autumn Term 2001

We will take into account key stage, GCSE and other outcomes from June/August 2001 in considering pupil progress. We will set new objectives and discuss future professional development activities. A new individual plan will be completed for each teacher.

The review process will inform our school management policies, the Education Development Plan and the School

Development Plan for financial years and academic years 2001/2002 and 2002/2003 (especially the costs of the development/training discussed in reviews).

[The introduction of the Education Development Plan in this section seems out of place as this is the term given to the planning work of an LEA, not a school.]

[Remember the words in ordinary type are only guidance. It is up to the governors to see if there is a better annual cycle for your school.]

6. PERFORMANCE MANAGEMENT CYCLE

Performance is set in the context of our school's plans for development, against the background of the local education development plan (EDP), national and local initiatives on improving teaching and any recent OFSTED report for the school.

Performance Management is an ongoing cycle, not an event, involving 3 stages of planning, monitoring performance and reviewing performance. The end of year review and Stage 1 may happen at the same time.

Stage 1: Planning

Each teacher will discuss and agree objectives with their team leader and record these in an individual plan (an example of a blank individual plan is attached at Annex B). Objectives should be challenging but realistic and take account of a teacher's job description and their existing skill and knowledge base.

There can be no hard and fast rule about how many objectives there should be for a teacher but we expect a minimum of three and no more that 5 or 6 to be agreed. Agreeing objectives does not mean itemising every activity but picking out key expectations and yardsticks. The range of objectives should match the nature of the job, including leadership or management areas as appropriate. Where someone has a wide range of managerial duties, objectives might focus on specific areas of this work.

Teacher objectives will cover pupil progress as well as ways of developing and improving teachers' professional practice. Leadership group staff and those with management allowances will have objectives relating to their additional responsibilities. **The head's objectives will cover school leadership and management as well as pupil progress.**

We will follow the following principles in discussing objectives:

- the team leader should ensure that the teacher understands what his or her objectives involve, is in a position to achieve them, knows what they need to do to achieve them and understands when and how they will be reviewed;
- objectives are written clearly and concisely and are measurable;
- objectives focus on issues/matters over which a teacher has direct influence/control and take into account fully the wider socio-economic, cultural and other external influences on pupils;
- objectives for each teacher should relate to the objectives in the school development plan and any departmental or team plans as well as to his or her own professional needs.

The leader should record the objectives which will apply for the review period. These should be jointly agreed. If there are any differences of opinion about the objectives, the teacher may add comments to the written record of objectives. If the head and the governing body representatives are unable to agree objectives, the governors appointed to review the performance of the head should set and record the objectives. The head may add comments to the written record of objectives.

Professional development opportunities are needed to support agreed objectives, to develop strengths and address areas for development or professional growth. The development page of the individual plan will be used to record action.

[The above sketches out a reasonable starting-point for discussion. Areas of uncertainty will emerge. For example, is the pupil progress measure for the head to refer to the progress of pupils he or she happens to teach, or to the school as a whole? If it is the latter, how can this be reconciled with the requirement that the objective should relate to a matter over which the reviewee has direct control?]

[It is not clear to what extent in the second cycle of review the objectives will be the same or different. Having to find up to six new objectives each year will become difficult over time unless they are very narrow and specific. Consider keeping to 3 or 4 as a maximum.]

Stage 2: Monitoring Progress

The teacher and team leader will keep progress under active review throughout the year using classroom observation and other relevant information. They will discuss any supportive action needed and keep development plans up-to-date.

The team leader should consult the teacher before seeking to obtain information, written or oral, relevant to the teacher's performance from other people.

Classroom observation is accepted good practice with a minimum of one observation each year required by Regulations. It is not a requirement to observe headteachers with teaching responsibilities. In our school we have agreed to have one full lesson observation per year, supplemented by any fuller observation of whole or part lesson which are agreed to be useful for developmental purposes.

In planning observation, we will follow these principles:

- successful observation requires preparation and training, and a clear understanding on the part of the teacher and team leader of its purpose;
- the nature of the observation will depend on its purpose;
- it is important that the observer ensures that the lesson proceeds in as normal an atmosphere as possible;
- full, constructive and timely feedback offers an opportunity to discuss what went well, what might be done better or differently next time. When giving feedback, the team leader should take into account the range of activities carried out by the teachers and the time spent on each activity.

[We will use the standard DfEE proforma for observations as attached at Annex C. Copies should be kept by the teacher and the team leader.]

[The use of the phrase "development plans" in the third line of this section is confusing. Development plans are normally taken to be school development plans and the plans for teachers are known as "individual plans".]

[Although it is not a requirement for a teaching head to be observed in the classroom, a head could ask for his or her own teaching to be part of the review process. In this case, the governors would have to request an observation from another relevant member of staff.]

[In practice, it is the "other relevant information" which will be the focus of discussion. This might include lesson plans, the completion of internal grading, the marking of exercise books or assessments, attendance, punctuality, evaluation of the quality of report-writing and administrative efficiency. The requirement that objectives should be measurable may be problematic in some of these examples but if the overall purpose of performance management is to raise standards, then issues such as these need to be addressed in the case of some teachers.]

Stage 3: Reviewing Performance

The annual review of the teacher's performance will use the recorded objectives as a focus to discuss his or her achievements and identify any development needs. It will be combined with agreeing objectives for the following performance management cycle.

[The recommendation in the previous sentence may turn out to be impractical, particularly at the end of the first cycle. The reviewee may well feel better for having a time to reflect on the process before embarking on the new cycle. As experience of the process improves, it may be possible to review and plan ahead in the same meeting.]

The focus of the review is on how to raise performance and improve effectiveness. It will involve:

- reviewing, discussing and confirming the teacher's essential tasks and objectives
- recognising strengths and achievements and taking account of factors outside the teacher's control
- confirming action agreed with the teacher at other reviews
- identifying areas for development and how these will be met
- recognising personal development needs *and*
- agreeing new clear objectives and completing an individual plan for the year ahead.

The team leader should evaluate the teacher's overall performance, including an assessment of the extent to which objectives have been met, and the teacher's contribution to the life of the school during the review period. It should take account of the stage the teacher is at in his or her career e.g. teacher with 2-3 years service, advanced skills teacher, senior manager.

Within 10 days of the review meeting, the team leader will prepare a written review statement recording the main points made at the review and the conclusions reached, included any identified development needs and activities recorded in a separate annex (but forming part of) the review statement. Once written, the team leader will give the teacher a copy of the statement. The teacher may within 10 days of first having access to the statement, add to is comments in writing. Good practice shows that the review statement should written as soon as possible after the review, whilst the facts are still fresh in the team leader's memory.

[Stage 3 is clearly the most delicate and challenging part of the whole process, especially for the team leader. An assessment of the "extent to which

objectives have been met" will invite judgements such as "fully met", "just met", "nearly met", "nowhere near met" but how to interpret these judgments may require some inter-team leader discussion if certain reviewees within a school are not going to feel disadvantaged by the perceived severity of their team leader.]

[How the cost of "identified development needs" is to be met remains one of the unresolved issues of this policy. As a guideline figure, If every teacher in the country identified a "need" which could be met by one day of release and attendance at a one-day course, the national cost would be over £120 million per year. "Needs" will be met in a variety of ways and some may not cost much money but others will be very much more expensive to provide than the benchmark figure of one day.]

7. LINKS BETWEEN PAY, CAREER STAGES AND PERFORMANCE MANAGEMENT

Induction - the final review meeting of the induction period can be used to agree objectives and professional development opportunities as the first stage of the teacher's subsequent performance management cycle; (Circular No: 5/99, The Induction Period for Newly Qualified Teachers, para. 58).

Information from the performance review statement can be used to inform aspects of the new pay structure from September 2000.

- Up to the Threshold — teachers can expect an annual increment if they are performing satisfactorily. Double increments for exceptional performance would need to be justified by review outcomes.
- Threshold — teachers who want to move to the upper pay spine should fill out the application form provided by the DfEE. Evidence from reviews will be used to inform applications by teachers and assessment by heads.
- Performance Pay Points above the threshold, Advanced Skills Teachers and teachers in the leadership group — performance reviews will form part of the evidence which schools can use to make decisions about awarding performance pay points to eligible teachers.

[There is no direct and automatic link between the review and pay. This not a bonus scheme for good work.]

[The double increment would have to be met from within the school's normal resources and would not be separately funded (see Appendix 4). After the initial period, so would any pay enhancement for other the other categories of teachers mentioned.]

8. MANAGING WEAK PERFORMANCE

Good management, with clear expectations and appropriate support, will go a long way towards identifying and handling weaknesses in performance.

The review meeting and review statement do not form part of any formal disciplinary or capability procedures. However, relevant information **from review statements may be taken into account by those who have access to them in making decisions and in advising those responsible for taking decisions, or making recommendations about performance, pay, promotion dismissal or disciplinary matters.**

9. CONFIDENTIALITY

The individual plan and the review statement are personal and confidential documents and should be kept in a secure place. The principles and provisions of the Data Protection Act 1998 should be followed at all times by those who have access to the documents.

[Although the above paragraph is not printed in bold italics, it is sufficiently clear and specific as to warrant inclusion unamended.]

10. ACCESS TO OUTCOMES

There will only be two copies of the review statement — one held by the teacher and another held by the head on a central file, to which the team leader or governors responsible for making decisions regarding pay could request access. A copy of the head's review statement should go to the chair of governors.

Information about performance review should be made available as listed below:

- the head should ensure that individual training and development needs are reflected in the school development plan and the programme for professional development
- **the head should ensure that training and development needs from the review statement are given to the person responsible for training and development at the school**
- **the head should report annually to the governing body on performance management in the school, including the effectiveness of the performance management procedures in the school, and the training and development needs of teachers and**

- **the CEO can request from the Chair of Governors a summary of the performance assessment section of the head's review statement**

The head should keep review statements for at least three years.

[It is difficult to see how the head could reflect individual training needs in the school development plan without breaching confidentiality. The best he or she may be able to achieve is a bland statement to the effect that "50% of the identified development needs will be met".]

[The head is required to report on the "effectiveness of the performance management review procedures" even though this will itself probably be one of the objectives of the head, at least in the fist cycle or two. This suggests that the governors should put in place some other criteria than the head's judgement on effectiveness.]

COMPLAINTS — THE REVIEW

Within 10 days of receiving the review statement:

- **Teachers can record their dissatisfaction with aspects of the review on the review statement. Where these cannot be resolved with the team leader, they can raise their concerns with the head. Where the head is the team leader, the teacher can raise the issue with the chair of governors.**
- **Headteachers can record their dissatisfaction with aspects of the review on the review statement. Where these cannot be resolved with the appointed governors, they can raise their concerns with the chair of governors. Where the chair of governors has been involved in the review process, the governing body should appoint one or more governors who have not participated in the head's review to act as review officer. No governor who is a teacher or staff member can be involved in performance review.**
- **The review officer (who could be the head, chair of governors or the governors appointed by the governing body) will investigate the complaint and take account of comments made by the job holder. The review officer should conduct a review of the complaint within 10 working days of referral. He or she may decide that the review statement should remain unchanged or may add any observations of his or her own. The review officer may decide, with the agreement of the person responsible for carrying out the initial review, or in the head's case all the appointed governors, to amend the review statement; or declare that the review statement is void and order a new review or part of the review to be repeated. Where**

a new review is ordered, new governors will be appointed to carry out the review of the headteacher. For teaches, the headteacher will appoint a new team leader. Any new review or part review ordered should be conducted within a further 15 days.

[This section is mandatory and cannot be altered, but it leaves many questions unanswered: What happens if the reviewee is dissatisfied with the second review? How many complaints can be made? What happens if the initial reviewer does not give his or her agreement to the proposed amendment? How can the review officer carry out a new review if he or she has not been taking part in the review process in-year? No doubt case law will establish the answers to these questions over the coming months.]

EVALUATION OF THE POLICY

The head shall provide an annual report to the governing body on how effective the performance management procedures have been.

As a school committed to ensuring that individual teachers, teams and the school continue to improve, the governing body and the head will check that effective and challenging objectives are set, that all reviews are completed on time and the assessment of performance is consistently applied in the school. We will evaluate the effectiveness of the policy in helping to improve standards of teaching and learning. As part of our ongoing commitment the governing body and the head will update and amend the documentation and the process as required, after consultation with all staff, to incorporate any major changes introduced either by the DfEE or the school to ensure that the policy is up-to-date and effective in our school.

[This must surely be an area of work where the governing body exercises its strategic and oversight role. Although the head will be required to provide the annual report, the governing body will want to draw evidence on the effectiveness of the policy from a wider range of sources, including the teachers and team leaders. A sub-group of the Personnel Committee may consider devising a questionnaire to be completed by all staff to indicate their overall level of satisfaction with the procedures. An even more radical approach would be to survey the parents and pupils to see if they have detected any difference in the school as a result of performance management.]

APPENDIX 3

RECOMMENDED READING

A Best Practice Model Performance Management Policy for All Schools, jointly produced by the Secondary Heads Association and the NASUWT. Copies available from:

- SHA, 130 Regent Road, Leicester, LE1 7PG, e-mail: info@sha.org.uk
- NASUWT, Hillscourt Education Centre, Rose Hill, Rednal, Birmingham, B45 8RSE-mail: nasuwt@mail.nasuwt.org.uk

APPENDIX 4

FUNDING THE PERFORMANCE MANAGEMENT POLICY

THE THRESHOLD PAYMENT

The government has committed itself to finding the money to pay the salary enhancement of all teachers who cross the threshold on to the upper pay spine. There is no quota and assessors are directed to apply clear criteria rather than to pass or fail pre-determined proportions. It is estimated that 250,000 teachers are eligible and it appears that about 80% of them have chosen to apply. If 80% of the applicants are successful, the cost in the first full financial year will be £380 million. Added to that will be the costs of the leadership spine assimilation. In the second year there will be a further round of successful applicants, probably adding a further £50 million to the second year of £380 million for the first cohort of those crossing the threshold. The Government will be well on the way to spending its promised £1 billion.

The cost of the threshold enhancement will be met in full by central government. At the end of the verification, the assessor and headteacher will sign a form listing the names of the successful applicants, send it to the LEA which will forward the details to the DfEE. The pro rata equivalent (seven twelfths for the months September 2000 to March 2001) of £2001 plus on-costs (superannuation and National Insurance contributions) will be added to the school's budget by the LEA which will recoup the money from central government.

The enhancement will also be funded in full by the government for the financial year 2001-2002 and the same mechanism will be used. It is not yet known how this extra money will be channelled to schools from the year 2002–2003. The government is committed to maintaining the enhanced funding, but mechanics of the transfer to school budgets is not yet known, other than a general remark that it will go through the "normal processes".

This will be a cause of anxiety to governors of schools in poorly-funded areas of the country. If the extra money is simply put into the national pot and then distributed through the present inequitable distribution system, some schools would find it impossible to meet the salary costs. The government is aware of this dilemma and there is active consideration of a new methodology for the funding of schools.

FUNDING THE LEADERSHIP SPINE ASSIMILATION

Teachers who move on to the leadership spine will receive a pay increase of at least £2,000 so schools will; receive this figure (plus on-costs) by direct grant form the LEA. This will be for one year only and the extra money will be added to the Education Spending Settlement for future years. This could be bad news for less well-funded LEAs.

Given the likelihood that deputies will receive a pay increase, every school with a deputy head in post on 1 September 2000 will recieve £900 per deputy and a contribution of 60% towards the costs of any single performance points awarded to deputies or heads. In the following year, the grant will be 30% but there will be a further 60% available for any further promotions made. What happens after that is unknown.

THE COST OF EXTERNAL ASSESSORS AND ADVISORS

These costs are met by the contractors and are funded directly by central government. If the governors want to use an external adviser for more than eight hours in total, they will have to pay the extra themselves from school funds.

THE COST OF PERFORMANCE MANAGEMENT CONSULTANTS AND THRESHOLD ASSESSMENT TRAINING

These costs are met from the *Standards Fund Grant 35* and covers attendance at DfEE sponsored conferences, the purchase of services from approved consultants and the attendance of governors at approved training.

THE COST OF IMPLEMENTING THE PERFORMANCE MANAGEMENT POLICY

There will be a considerable time factor involved in the process of performance management and the government has earmarked funds for this in *Standards Fund Grant 35A*. It appears that the funds available will just about cover the supply costs for one teaching period (one hour) for a teacher to be observed. It must be expected that the interview process involved in performance management will be carried out in directed time when pupils are not present. This could present time-budget problems for team leaders who, as heads of department, already come close to the 1,265 hour maximum.

THE COST OF PROVIDING STAFF DEVELOPMENT IDENTIFIED BY THE PERFORMANCE MANAGEMENT POLICY

This the big unknown because it is an open-ended and uncostable development. Presumably schools will use Standards Fund grants to cover this but whether these will be large enough to meet the demand remains to be seen. For every teacher in the country to have just one day of training off-site would cost in the order of £800 million per year. If sums of this magnitude are not made available, the whole process could suffer the same fate as the previous appraisal system which fell into disrepute because the needs which had been identified could not be met.

By the time this pocket book is published, the government will have published its proposals to increase even further the amount of money in the Standards Fund and to simplify its administration.

APPENDIX 4

RECOMMENDED READING

Fairer Funding, Secondary Heads Association, 130 Regent Road, Leicester, LE1 7PG, £9.50

APPENDIX 5

THE THRESHOLD ASSESSMENT CRITERIA

Teachers have to provide evidence in relation to eight standards grouped into five broad areas.

1. PROFESSIONAL KNOWLEDGE AND UNDERSTANDING

This standard requires evidence that teachers have a thorough and up-to-date knowledge of the teaching of their subject(s) and take account of wide curriculum developments which are relevant to their work.

2. TEACHING AND ASSESSMENT

This group of standards seeks evidence that teachers:

- consistently and effectively plan lessons and sequences of lessons to meet pupils' individual learning needs
- consistently and effectively use a range of appropriate strategies for teaching and classroom management
- consistently and effectively use information about prior attainment to set well grounded expectations for pupils and monitor progress to give clear and constructive feedback.

3. PUPIL PROGRESS

As a result of the teachers' teaching, pupils achieve well relative to their prior attainment, making progress as good as or better than similar pupils nationally. This should be shown in marks or grades in any relevant national tests or examinations, or school-based assessment for pupils where national test and examinations are not taken.

4. WIDER PROFESSIONAL EFFECTIVENESS

Teachers should demonstrate that they:
- take responsibility for their professional development and use the outcomes to improve their teaching and pupils' learning
- make an active contribution to the policies and aspirations of the school.

5. PROFESSIONAL CHARACTERISTICS

The final area in which the teacher has to produce evidence repeats to some extent the previous ones but the teachers is asked to provide supplementary evidence if possible:

(a) Inspiring trust and confidence:
- showing an evident commitment to pupils and respect for others
- influencing others through integrity and professional confidence.

(b) Team Building:
- understanding others and using that understanding effectively
- contributing constructively to work teams
- rewarding achievement
- confronting issues that might hinder effective team-working.

(c) Engaging and motivating:
- getting classes or groups to work effectively together
- agreeing clear expectations with pupils
- reaching out to pupils for whom learning is not a natural avenue for progress
- making learning relevant and interesting.

(d) Analytical thinking:
- identifying cause and effect in pupils' learning
- recognising patterns in situations, making comparisons and links to gauge the best learning strategies.

(e) Take positive steps to improve the quality of pupils' learning, for example:
 - improving the way information or resources are gathered
 - anticipating difficulties and resolving problems before they become too far advanced.

The teacher fills in an application which is passed to the headteacher. The head then makes an individual judgement on whether or not each standard has been met and then gives an overall judgement, citing evidence which has been taken into account.

The headteacher's judgments are monitored by the external assessor.

Index

R

S